HARRIET TUBMAN

FOR BEGINNERS®

HARRIET TUBMAN

FOR BEGINNERS®

BY ANNETTE M. ALSTON
ILLUSTRATED BY LYNSEY HUTCHINSON

Foreword by Susan Ades Stone

FOR BEGINNERS®

For Beginners LLC
30 Main Street, Suite 303
Danbury, CT 06810 USA
www.forbeginnersbooks.com

A For Beginners® Documentary Comic Book
Copyright © 2017

Cataloging-in-Publication information is available from the Library of Congress.

ISBN # 978-1-939994-72-1 Trade

Manufactured in the United States of America

For Beginners® and Beginners Documentary Comic Books® are published by
For Beginners LLC.

First Edition

10 9 8 7 6 5 4 3 2 1

*To the two people who brought me into this world
and nurtured my love of reading and writing. And to all of the
largely male-dominated (father, uncles, brothers) family
political discussions in which I took part.*

Contents

~ Foreword ~

by Susan Ades Stone

W HAT MAKES A PERSON TRULY LEGENDARY— someone worthy of being enshrined not just in our history books, but on stamps, on street signs, and in the portrait galleries of our most august institutions? That was the question a colleague and I asked ourselves in 2014 as we inaugurated the advocacy organization Women On 20s and set out to convince the president, the Treasury secretary, and the American public that it was high time to honor a female American hero in the most exclusive national portrait gallery of all—our paper currency.

And who would it be? Of all the great women trailblazers who had innovated, inspired, led, persevered, and sacrificed to help shape a nation, which one should be elevated above all the rest and chosen as a symbol to the world of American values and culture? We wanted the public to help decide and be witness to historic change. And so, in a ten-week social media campaign that swept the nation and made headline news around the world, more than 600,000 people cast ballots. When the votes were tallied, the people's choice was Harriet Tubman.

Truth be told, she was my choice, too.

Before the campaign went live on March 1, 2015, my Women On 20s partner, Barbara Ortiz Howard, and I had narrowed the field, with the help of historians and others, from a list of 100 women who fit the Treasury Department criteria of being both deceased and somewhat known to the public for their accomplishments. Then I researched and wrote short biographies of the fifteen final candidates to be posted on our website, which would host an electronic ballot. We wanted to give each of the candidates an equal shot at winning votes by highlighting not just what was generally known about their remarkable lives, but by bringing into the foreground their lesser-known deeds and the challenges and hardships they endured. From the start, Barbara and I believed that even if we failed in our mission to get a woman's portrait on the $20 bill, we would have succeeded if we could get a national conversation going about recognizing and valuing the contributions of great American women—not only those whose names most of us have heard, like Eleanor Roosevelt, Rosa Parks, Susan B. Anthony, Clara Barton, and, yes, Harriet Tubman, but others who remain relatively obscure in our history lessons, like Alice Paul, Frances Perkins, and Barbara Jordan.

Each time I tried to summarize a candidate's life and accomplishments in a mere 500 words, I would say to myself, "Okay, the others were amazing, but this one tops them all." Then I came to Harriet Tubman, and the bar was raised to a new height that no one else seemed likely to scale. Like most Americans, I had known of her since grade-school days as a freed slave and conductor on the Underground Railroad. Now, suddenly, she was so much more—a lifelong fighter for freedom, equality, and humanitarian causes. In our rubric to rank possible candidates, we relied on two basic criteria: the impact the person had on society and the challenges she faced in making her mark, giving the former double weight. Again and again and again, Tubman hit it out of the park on both criteria.

After a five-week "primary" election, in which people were asked to record their top three picks, three candidates advanced to the final round. We had been hoping the new currency would debut in time to celebrate the centennial of women's suffrage in 2020, but, in an ironic twist, none of the three great suffragist leaders—Susan B. Anthony,

Elizabeth Cady Stanton, or Alice Paul—made the cut. (If their votes were added together, they would have taken the top spot over Eleanor Roosevelt.) Coming in second, Harriet Tubman had fought on the front lines of women's suffrage, as well as in the battle against slavery, and so we looked to her to carry that flag. Civil rights icon Rosa Parks claimed the third spot on the ballot.

In the ten weeks of final polling, the American public clearly did its homework. Teachers coast-to-coast, from kindergarten through college, brought women's history to life by engaging with students in the Women On 20s campaign. Our website recorded more than two million visitors, who collectively viewed more than nine million pages of history and information. Many visitors took to social media to promote their favorite candidates. State houses and city halls introduced resolutions plugging their hometown heroines. And bills were introduced in Congress mandating a woman's portrait on the $20 bill by 2020.

The ultimate winner of the poll, Harriet Tubman, was a fitting choice to replace President Andrew Jackson, who, while a charismatic leader and patriot, was also a slave trader, oppressor of Native Americans, and weak ambassador for the values of social justice and equality promoted both at home and abroad. Tubman was a woman for all ages, and her victory was cheered on both sides of the political aisle. Her many missions presaged social movements that occupy us today, showing by example that black lives matter, as do the lives of women, the elderly, the infirm, and the voiceless. Had she been male, her accomplishments would have been remarkable indeed. But because Tubman was female *and* a woman of color, her accomplishments rose to the level of the extraordinary. She needed to be reintroduced to the world as, yes, a conductor of the Underground Railroad and the Moses of her people, but also as a Joan of Arc, Martin Luther King, Susan B. Anthony, and Mother Teresa all rolled into one.

On April 20, 2016, US Treasury Secretary Jacob Lew made it official. Harriet Tubman would be the woman to break the paper ceiling, her portrait to appear on the $20 bill in place of Jackson's. The design, he said, would be unveiled on the 100th anniversary of women's suffrage in 2020. Immediately, Tubman's name started trending on social media. She became the most Googled subject of the moment, only to be surpassed by the musician Prince, whose tragic death was reported the next day.

The Women on 20s website (http://www.womenon20s.org) remains active as a resource for anyone seeking a peek into a grassroots campaign for historic change seeded by just a few determined people; the Library of Congress has also captured its pages as part of the public record. Beyond the meager 500 words I wrote about Harriet Tubman for that campaign—Tubman the escaped slave, Underground Railroad conductor, abolitionist, wartime nurse, Union spy, suffragist, humanist, and ordinary woman—a remarkably rich backstory is compellingly and beautifully told in the book you are now holding. The pages that follow offer a detailed and colorful picture of a woman who was rarely photographed, having lived much of her life on the run and shunning the limelight. Diving deep into her story, you can't help but feel her humanity, still so alive today. By the time you turn the final pages, I'm sure that you, like me, will feel great pride in seeing Harriet Tubman take her place among the great Americans memorialized in our pantheon of paper money.

Susan Ades Stone is an award-winning journalist who served as executive director and campaign strategist for Women On 20s, the nonprofit organization that lobbied successfully for the appearance of a woman on the front of the $20 bill and that conducted the public election that nominated Harriet Tubman.

Introduction

MOST AMERICANS LEARNED ABOUT HARRIET TUB-
man as schoolchildren. We came to know her as a runaway
slave who found freedom in the North in the era before
the Civil War. And we learned that she was not content in her freedom
until she went back several more times to free family members and
other slaves. Exactly how many more times she attempted the mission
and how many slaves she led to freedom are still not known for sure,
but the fact that she went back at all—risking capture and a return to
slavery, if not worse—raised her to heroic stature. She became known
as "the Moses of Her People," attaining legendary status. She was the
most memorable conductor on the Underground Railroad, and her
exploits rose to mythic level.

> *"I have heard their groans and sighs, and seen their
> tears, and I would give every drop of blood in my veins
> to free them."* —HARRIET TUBMAN

In 2016, the US Treasury announced that Tubman had been
selected as the first woman to appear on the front of US paper currency, replacing President Andrew Jackson on the $20 bill. (Jackson
would be moved to the back.) Tubman had been selected over such

other historic figures as First Lady Eleanor Roosevelt, civil rights pioneer Rosa Parks, women's suffrage leaders Susan B. Anthony and Elizabeth Cady Stanton, fellow abolitionist Sojourner Truth, and others.

The Harriet Tubman National Historical Park, at her former home and church in Auburn, New York, was officially established in January 2017. The Harriet Tubman Underground Railroad National Monument, an 11,750-acre unit of the National Park Service on Maryland's Eastern Shore, was designated in 2013. And the state of Maryland opened its Harriet Tubman Underground Railroad State Park and Visitor Center in Dorchester County in March 2017.

Also in 2013, the hundredth anniversary of her death, agencies of the US and Canadian governments, UNESCO, and a host of civic organizations created a variety of new educational resources to help the general public learn more about Tubman and her era.[1]

Museums and memorials established across the United States over the years pay tribute to the Moses of Her People.

❖ ❖ ❖

So what was it about Harriet Tubman that raised her to the status of national icon? Who was the *real* Harriet Tubman? Or maybe the better questions are:

- **What does she represent to us as Americans?**
- **What does her story tell us about our history, heritage, and national identity?**

In order to answer these questions, we need to start at the beginning of her life, which in many ways is rooted in the genesis of American life. Is the United States ready to come fully to terms with the gritty and hard-to-face aspects of its early history? Is the image of Harriet Tubman on the $20 bill a long overdue statement to that effect? Are we really prepared to come to terms with "America's Original Sin"—the Middle Passage and institution of slavery? For indeed the foundation of American society and its capitalist system carries many scars, which run as deep as those on a slave's back.

A biography of Harriet Tubman may have been the first book I pulled from the shelves of the public library and took home to read. I was in second grade. Most children's biographies of her were based on two works by Sarah Hopkins Bradford, going back to 1869 *(Scenes From the Life of Harriet Tubman)* and 1886 *(Harriet, the Moses of Her People)*. Biographers and historians since then have

3

shown that there were some embellishments to her life's story that originated in these early works. While the exaggerations do not take away from Tubman's real-life accomplishments, they began a process that elevated her to a mythic status nearly comparable to that of John Henry or Paul Bunyan. The real Harriet Tubman was very much an ordinary woman with extraordinary faith, talent, and drive.

Beyond the myth, Tubman's story was perhaps the first to transcend the confines of "Black History" as it was traditionally taught in the broader context of American History. For it has come to be recognized that Tubman's struggle for the promise of freedom, individuality, life, liberty, and the pursuit of happiness was no different from that of the men who signed the Declaration of Independence or the Constitution of the United States. Tubman is well understood as the midwife of American democracy, completing the birth process started almost one hundred years before when Thomas Jefferson penned, "All men are created equal." Her roles in the Underground Railroad and Civil War helped end slavery in America, as her efforts as a suffragist and humanitarian looked to higher ideals.

> *"The midnight sky and the silent stars have been the witness of your devotion to freedom and of your heroism."* —FREDERICK DOUGLASS

This book does three things. It portrays the true Harriet Tubman—the woman behind the myth. It describes the environment and society that created her and in which she lived. And it offers a fuller understanding and appreciation of the outsize influence that this five-foot woman, born into slavery, had on the evolution of the United States.

Harriet Tubman For Beginners begins with the circumstances of her birth, her family, and her life as an enslaved African in Maryland.

It follows Harriet as she grows into a young woman, how she defines and redefines herself, gains her freedom, and expands her dream by assisting family members and others in escaping bondage.

We see how religion—an early brand of black liberation theology—was entrenched in her life and how it influenced her decisions and actions.

We learn about her relationship with the radical abolitionist John Brown (who dubbed her "The General"), her role in the insurrection he organized, and other forms of resistance being pursued by abolitionists in those volatile times.

We discover some of the lesser-known roles Tubman played during the Civil War—nurse, cook, and spy for the Union cause—and her work during Reconstruction and beyond to support women's suffrage, her church, and loved ones. By her later years, the "Moses of Her People" and "The General" had earned a change in her unofficial title to "Auntie Harriet."

The book concludes with a look at some contemporary portrayals, Tubman's place in the pantheon of American historical figures, the process of mythmaking and history, and an assessment of this remarkable woman's meaning to blacks, women, the pursuit of social justice, and the collective national consciousness to the present day.

And so it is hoped that *Harriet Tubman For Beginners* helps mark the beginning of a field that must be known as Tubman Studies.

—Annette Alston

1

"Minty" Ross, Her Family, and Slave Life in Antebellum Maryland

> *"[I]f her weary head dropped, and her head ceased to rock the cradle, the child would cry out and then down would come the whip upon the face and neck of the poor weary creature. The scars are still plainly visible where they cut into the flesh."*
> —SARAH H. BRADFORD
> *Scenes in the Life of Harriet Tubman*

IN 2005, TWO GREAT-GRANDNIECES OF HARRIET TUBMAN had an opportunity to travel to Ghana, West Africa, where they believe the seed of their genealogy in America was sown. Here they would complete the circle that started in the early to mid-1700s when Modesty, an Ashanti girl, was ripped from her tribe in or near Accra, Ghana, and brought to the American colonies. She was eventually purchased by Atthow Pattison, a successful landowner and slaveholder in southeast Maryland's Dorchester County. Records indicate that Modesty was the mother of Harriet "Rit" Green, who would become the mother of Harriet Tubman.

Geography is always important in understanding the course of history and, in this case, the struggles that precipitated the decisions made by the enslaved and slave owners. Here the setting is southeastern Maryland and the land settled and owned by white slaveholding families. Maryland's proximity to the North—the Mason-Dixon Line formed its border with Pennsylvania beginning in the 1760s—made the structure of slavery in that colony different from most others, particularly those farther south that relied on labor-intensive cotton.

Modesty and Baby Rit

Landowners in the Dorchester region appeared to have a simple formula for growth that turned into an unwritten rule: marry within the area to amass wealth. As a way of increasing their property holdings and status, white landed gentry would intermarry with other estate owners in the region. Over the generations, the leading families on Maryland's Eastern Shore consolidated control over vast expanses of rich farmland, forests, and marsh areas.

Harriet's family from the time of Modesty was intricately involved with four white families in the Dorchester region: the Pattisons, the Thompsons, the Brodesses, and the Stewarts. As the landed white families merged, shifted, and expanded their estates, African American slave families were moved around the regional network. By the 19th century, black family units were interwoven among Dorchester's landed white families, creating a large network of interaction and communication

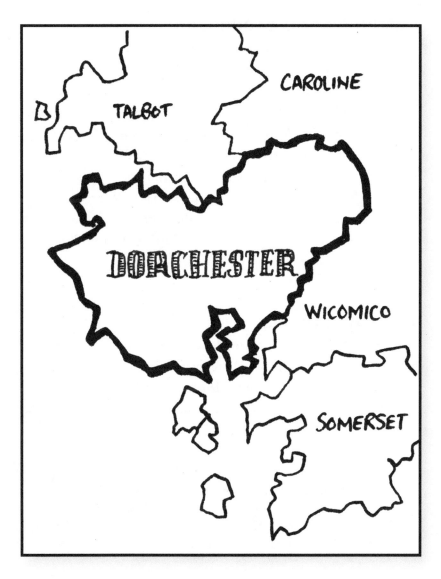

throughout the area. Enslaved blacks often worked alongside free black men at the docks or in skilled labor markets, sharing information and extending the network over time.

The interrelations among blacks and white, and the relationships among the area's white families, created the setting and cast of characters for the drama that was to come.

Pattisons and Brodesses

In 1776, the year the Continental Congress signed the Declaration of Independence less than 150 miles to the north, Atthow Pattison's 265-acre estate in Dorchester County included five slaves. Modesty, the grandmother of Harriet Tubman, is believed to be one of them. By 1790 the number enslaved had increased to seven; Rit, Tubman's mother, was born into the household sometime between 1785 and 1789. Upon Pattison's death in 1797, ownership of Rit passed to his granddaughter, Mary Pattison. Three years later, Mary went on to marry Joseph Brodess, a local farmer in the central Dorchester town of Bucktown. On June 14, 1801, Mary gave birth to Edward Brodess; a little more than a year later, Joseph Brodess died.

The Thompsons

Anthony Thompson was a moderately successful and respected businessman and landowner whose family lineage went back to the founders of Dorchester County. He considered himself a benevolent caretaker because of his promise of manumission for the loyalty and

MANUMISSION: the act of freeing enslaved persons voluntarily, or the document that legally granted freedom. The motivations for freeing the enslaved were varied—inability to support them, arrangements for the enslaved to "purchase themselves," or, in rare instances, benevolence.

good behavior of those he held in bondage. His wife, Polly King, died between 1800 and 1803, leaving him with three sons under the age of 15—Edward, Anthony, and Absalom. Thompson owned nine slaves; one of them was Ben Ross, who was to become the father of Harriet Tubman.

In keeping with the unwritten formula for regional expansion, the recently widowed Anthony Thompson and the recently widowed Mary Brodess married in 1803 and consolidated their assets. Mary Brodess brought her son, Edward, and her personal slave, Rit, along with four enslaved males that had belonged to her deceased husband.

The Stewarts

The Stewarts appeared to be a family of mixed ideals. Joseph Stewart, Anthony Thompson, and Robert Tubman were among the county commissioners who oversaw the operations of the Black Water and Parsons Creek Canal Company, set up to expand the shipment of goods across the area's extensive waterways. The project was completed in the 1830s after twenty years of effort and named the Stewart Canal. Joseph's son, James A. Stewart, was the Pattison family attorney, a businessman, and later a US congressman. He was a major slaveholder and is not recorded as having manumitted any of them. (His brother, John T. Stewart, later hired a teenaged Harriet Tubman.) Joseph's brother Levin, however, went to court and turned in documents to manumit all of his enslaved at specified ages. Levin's friend James Pattison did the same a year later. These and other manumissions during the 1850s helped develop a free black community in Dorchester County.

To be clear, Levin's actions were hardly the norm. Even though he had less need for slaves than area farmers because he was going into the shipbuilding and trading business with his brother in Georgetown, he could have sold his slaves for top dollar to a Baltimore or New Orleans trader. Instead, he sold or gave them to his brothers, who honored the manumission schedules after his death in 1825.

Masters and the Enslaved

The master-slave relationship may have seemed complicated on one level, but it was quite simple on another.

While it appears that a few slave owners were moved by the soaring sermons of Quakers and preachers to appease their consciences by promising manumission to their human chattel, more were motivated to do so by the shifting tide from agriculture to industry on the Eastern Shore. Most, however, kept their enslaved despite declining need. Owners often found they could make more money on a slave by hiring him or her out to local farmers and businessmen than they could by selling them to a New Orleans or Mississippi slave trader. It also paid for slave owners to create incentives for their African forced laborers to remain loyal and dependent, thereby avoiding the cost and aggravation of tracking runaways or losing their property altogether.

Still, the enslaved in the Chesapeake region faced the constant threat of being sold into the Deep South and losing contact with family members forever. The threat of permanent, distant separation was especially acute wherever a slave owner's business was not thriving. Black families were considered fortunate if their loved ones were sold or transferred by marriage or inheritance to another white owner in the region. Only the lucky were granted the privilege of hiring themselves out by their owners, typically for an annual fee. This gave enslaved men and women the opportunity to "moonlight" and, over time, buy their own freedom.

When it came to buying one's freedom, however, time was a major obstacle. If a black man managed to buy his own freedom over a period of years—which it often took—he might not have time to buy freedom for his wife and children before they were sold on the auction block. The same held true for a free black man who married an enslaved woman. The children of the marriage took on the status of the mother rather than that of the father. And so, even when freedom was a real possibility for the African American man, he did not control the fate of his wife or children. The slave owner could decide to sell them or keep them at any time. How free was a man if someone else could determine the destiny of his loved ones?

Slavery may not have seemed as harsh in Maryland as it was in other parts of the country—especially where cotton was king—but it was still a living hell, with the constant threat of being dragged deeper into the pit of the South. Less complicated than all the conditions and limitations of manumission was the simple fact that a slave owner did whatever he deemed in his own best interest and that of his family, rather than that of the enslaved and enslaved family.

And yet, while hiring out their human property seemed advantageous for Maryland slaveholders at the time, they did not take full account of the connections developing among the region's farms and other workplaces. A growing network of free blacks, hired enslaved, and mariners along the Eastern Shore was forming in preparation for the escapes that were to take place just as Harriet Tubman was coming into the world.

Harriet is Born

Ben Ross was skilled in lumber inspection and managed the timber operations of the Thompson estate. He was one of only a few of Thompson's forty slaves who was promised land upon his manumission at age 45.

When Mary Brodess inherited Harriet "Rit" Green from her grandfather, Atthow Pattison, in 1797, the terms of his will stipulated that his slave women were to be manumitted at the age of 45. Actually realizing the terms of the bequest, however, depended on certain factors. Docu-

AGE OF MANUMISSION

One way of ensuring slave loyalty was to promise manumission at a given age, usually 45. In Maryland it was against the law to manumit a slave after the age of 45, which was seen as neglect. The median life span of a slave was 21, compared to 45 for a white man. Slave owners would often manumit slaves who were too old to work and therefore too old to care for themselves or hire themselves out. The Maryland law was enacted to prevent that from happening.

ments had to be filed properly in the courts, and the evidence had to remain intact. (In fact, some records in the Dorchester courthouse were later destroyed by fire, with no backups in the state house.) Finally, the secondary owner, being aware that the slave was to be set free at a certain age, had to resist the temptation to sell the slave out of state before he/she came of age. (Technically it was illegal to sell a "term slave" out of state, but it did happen. Harriet's parents would experience the pain of such a sale at least twice and would face the threat multiple times afterwards.)

The merging of Brodess and Thompson properties in 1803 brought together Ben Ross and Rit Green—the parents of Harriet Tubman. They were married within the next five years, and by 1824 they had had six or seven children together.

Recent research has shown that Anthony Thompson paid a midwife $2 to assist Rit Green in childbirth on March 15, 1822. The baby may well have been Harriet Tubman, believed to have been born on the Thompson estate south of Madison, near the Blackwater River. She was named Araminta "Minty" Ross, probably after an aunt. Like most enslaved people, Harriet would never know her birthdate for sure. All they knew was the approximate year and maybe the season; if they were fortunate, they could pin down the month.

While Harriet apparently was born on the Thompson plantation, she was actually the property of his stepson, Edward Brodess. Thompson had raised Edward along with his own four children after Mary's passing around 1810. When Edward came of age, he inherited the property that had been his mother's and eventually married.

Brodess was not as wealthy as his stepfather or Thompson's own sons, and there was a rift between them. Thompson had taken Brodess to court for money he believed Brodess owed him for building on the Bucktown estate Edward had inherited. Apparently the Brodesses felt the financial sting of farm life on the Eastern Shore. In 1825, about a year after marrying Eliza Anne Keene, Edward Brodess sold one of Keene's slaves, 15-year-old James, and one of his own slaves, 16-year-old Rhody (believed to be Mariah Ritty, Rit and Ben's daughter), to a trader from Mississippi.

Sixteen-year-old Mariah and fifteen-year-old James torn from their family and friends forever

Enslaved Child

Like so many other landowners in the area, Edward Brodess also began hiring out his slaves. One of Harriet Tubman's earliest memories was being four or five years old and minding her younger brother and an infant—perhaps a niece or nephew—while her mother was cooking at the "big house." With everyone else working or being hired out, five-year-old Minty Ross was left the responsibility of baby care. She later recounted the experience:

> *I used to be in a hurry for her* [her mother] *to go, so's I could play the baby was a pig in a bag, and hold him up by the bottom of his dress. I had a nice frolic with that baby, swinging him all around his feet in the dress and his little head and arms touching the floor. Because I was too small to hold him higher. It was late nights before my mother got home, and when he'd get worrying, I'd cut a fat chunk of pork and toast it on the coals and put it in his mouth. One night he went to sleep with that hanging out, and when my mother come home she thought I'd done kill him. I nursed that there baby till he was so big I couldn't tote him any mo'.*[2]

Apparently taking care of her baby relatives at the age of four or five gave Minty enough experience to be rented out by age seven. A woman named Miss Susan, newly married and with a baby, was especially cruel to young Minty, keeping a whip by her pillow to lash the girl if she stopped rocking the cradle and the baby cried.

Minty growing up under the threat of a whip

Many times during her childhood labors, Minty returned home in worse condition than when she left. At the age of about seven, she was rented out to one James Cook and his wife, who charged her with retrieving muskrats from traps in a nearby swamp. Trapping was often conducted in the winter months, when the pelts were at their peak. Minty was expected to wade through freezing water to retrieve the muskrats, and she became deathly sick.

Minty retrieving muskrats in the bitter cold

Restored to health by her mother, Minty was rented out again. Many years later she recounted an incident in which she was beaten badly—again by Miss Susan—because she had begun dusting the furniture before all the dust had settled from sweeping the floor. Her slave cabin had a dirt floor and no furniture, and she had never been taught to dust. As Harriet Tubman, she carried those scars for the rest of her life.

Minty wore the scars from her early child-hood beatings for the rest of her life.

As a teenager of about 15, Minty witnessed a black man running away from his overseer. The slavemaster caught up with him at a dry goods store and asked Minty to help tie him up. The girl didn't move. When the runaway slave slipped away and began running again, the overseer picked up a heavy iron weight and threw it at him. The object struck Minty in the head instead, sinking deep into her scalp and

After the head injury, Minty often had visions of flying like a bird.

exposing her skull. She was carried back to the Barnett home where she had been rented out and laid on the loom seat, unconscious and with no medical attention for days. Later, she recounted, she was sent out to the fields to work with sweat and blood still pouring from her head. Eventually the injury so debilitated her that she was sent back to the Brodess farm, where the family tried to sell her. No one was interested because of the injury.

Once again her mother nursed her back to health, though the long-term effects ran deeper than the scars on her skin. For the rest of her life, Minty/Harriet suffered from a type of epilepsy that manifested itself in sudden sleeping spells and fainting episodes.

> "I grew up like a neglected weed, ignorant of liberty, having no experience of it. Then I was not happy or contented: every time I saw a white man I was afraid of being carried away." —HARRIET TUBMAN

Sometimes she would fall asleep in the middle of a conversation, then wake up and continue the conversation exactly where she had left off. On other occasions, she would fall into a deep sleep and not wake for hours. Also related to the seizures and sleeping spells were visions that often had religious significance. While all of these unexpected episodes created serious challenges and made certain situations even more precarious throughout her life, she also acknowledged that they helped guide her through some dangerous circumstances.

With all the overwork, physical abuse, and neglect she endured as a child and teenager, Minty Ross also lived in constant fear of being sold farther south, as two of her sisters had been.

2

Decisions: To Be Harriet,
Keeping Still While Moving

"There are two things I've got a right to, and these are Liberty or Death—one or the other I mean to have. No one will take me back alive." —HARRIET TUBMAN

T HOUGH MINTY ROSS, LATER HARRIET TUBMAN, would suffer from a form of epilepsy for the rest of her life, her physical strength improved so much that she was hired out as a teenager to Madison shipbuilder, merchant, and slave owner John T. Stewart (the son of Joseph Stewart and brother of James A. Stewart). Minty did work that was normally done by men, lugging barges down canals and pulling plows like oxen. Working alongside slaves as well as free men, she became part of a quiet network that had been made up exclusively of black males. This network included freedmen, slaves, and black mariners who exchanged information about (or from) distant families, the successful slave uprising against Napoleon's colonial forces in Saint Domingue (Haiti), and other news. There was always word of runaways, some successful and many not.

Marriage and the Call of Freedom

The expansion of industry and commerce on the Eastern Shore of Maryland often lent itself to hiring help rather than purchasing and housing slaves. With slave owners in the area making more money by hiring out their slaves, they had to trust their human chattel to travel sometimes long distances, stay for periods of days or weeks at a time, and then return. To build trust, as we have seen, many slaveholders made a promise of manumission by a certain age. Thus, as industry grew in southeastern Maryland, so did the number of free blacks. It was working within this network that brought Minty Ross into contact with John Tubman, a tall, dark mulatto born free to free parents in Dorchester County. He lived and worked in an area known as Peter's Neck, not far from where Minty's own father lived and worked.

In Tubman's time as a slave, it was not uncommon for a free man to marry an enslaved woman. The danger to such a family would be in bearing children, as any of their offspring would take on the status of the mother. Thus, when Minty Ross married John Tubman, a free man, they both knew that any children they had would belong to Edward Brodess. And so, during their five-year marriage, they had no children.

It was about the time of their marriage in 1844, when Minty changed her name to Harriet Tubman. Some believe she changed her name in honor of her mother, Harriet. Others believe the new name was part of a larger spiritual conversion. Either way, Harriet embraced a change in identity, focusing on freedom for her and her family. Her father, Ben, had been manumitted about four years before Harriet's marriage. Obviously he was a favorite of his owner, as he was granted ten acres of land for life as well as exclusive rights to all timber on the land. Such an arrangement was almost unheard of at the time, but Ben's wife Rit and his children remained enslaved!

Harriet Tubman, for her part, worked out a deal to pay Brodess an annual fee for the privilege of hiring herself out to landowners and businessmen of her choosing—by now a common practice on Maryland's Eastern Shore. Harriet made enough extra money to buy a pair of steers and hired herself out in off times for plowing, carting, and other heavy labor. In 1848–1849, however, illness prevented Harriet from working as often as she had, and the $50 or $60 she was paying Brodess per year was not enough. Brodess was running deeper into financial difficulty, and everyone on his plantation could feel the stress.

Fears and Prayers

All the while, the fear of being sold farther south hung over Harriet and the other slaves. Now it was becoming real. Two of Harriet's sisters, Linah and Soph, were set to be freed at the age of 45 according to their previous owner's will. Without real fear of consequences, however, Brodess illegally listed Linah and Soph as slaves for life and sold them out of state. Linah left behind two children, Kizziah (Kessiah) and Harriet, Tubman's nieces. It was only a matter of time before they and she, too, would be hoisted onto an auction block, sold, chained, and transported out of state. Harriet prayed constantly for Edward Brodess's heart to change.

I prayed all night long for master, till the first of March; and all the time he was bringing people to look at me, and trying to sell me. Then we hear that some us was going to be sold to go with the chain-gang down to the cotton and rice fields, and they said I was going and my brother and sisters.[1]

23

At that point, it was Harriet's prayer that changed:

Oh Lord, If you ain't never going to change that man's heart, kill him, Lord and take him out of the way.[2]

And that prayer was soon answered. On March 7, 1849, Edward Brodess was dead at the age of 47. Tubman was shaken by the suddenness of his passing. As she later recounted to biographer Sarah Bradford,

Next thing I heard old master was dead, and he died just as he lived. Oh, then, it appeared like I'd give all the world full of gold, if I had it, to bring that poor soul back. But I couldn't pray for him no longer.[3]

As it turned out, the death of Edward Brodess only escalated the very changes that Tubman feared most. He left all of his possessions except the slaves to his wife Eliza. In spite of his promise to set them free for good behavior, he bequeathed all of the slaves to his children, with no provision for manumission. The widow Eliza, financially strapped, petitioned the Dorchester County Orphans Court to sell some of the slaves to pay off the family debts.

In the meantime, not long after marrying, Harriet had hired an attorney for $5 to inquire into the will of her mother's former master, Atthow Pattison. Now the lawyer's findings may have prevented, or at least postponed, the immediate sale of Harriet and her other siblings. For it was discovered that Rit, Harriet's mother, had been set to be manumitted at the age of 45, as were any children bequeathed to Pattison's heirs. By the time of Edward Brodess's death, however, Rit was more than 60 years old and, under Maryland law, had passed the age that manumission was allowed. Because Edward Brodess, Atthow Pattison's great-grandson, had not abided by the terms of the will, Rit and her children were cheated out of the freedom that was promised them.

But Tubman's inquiry into the status of her mother also opened the door for a lawsuit by the Pattison family. In July 1849, soon after Brodess's death, the Pattison family sued his widow, Eliza, claiming ownership of Rit and any of her children over the age of 45; the lawsuit included a claim for any money earned from Rit's labor beginning at age 45. The upshot for Harriet and her siblings, at least for the time being, was that the case made it impossible for Eliza to sell any of Rit's children until the matter had been settled.

Not that these proceedings prevented Eliza from trying time and again. In August 1849, she and the estate administrator advertised the sale of Kizziah Bowley, Harriet's 25-year-old niece. Kizziah's husband John, a free black man who worked as a ship's carpenter, and his brother tried to work out a deal to buy her and won a temporary reprieve. Soon two of Tubman's other nieces went on the auction block, and this sale went through for $375 to a local merchant. Then a few weeks later, Eliza sold yet another slave from the family estate, Dawes Keene. Harriet saw the writing on the wall. She had to flee, even though it was against her husband's will and he refused to go with her.

Escape

Harriet and two of her brothers, Henry and Benjamin, fled the Caroline County plantation of Dr. Anthony C. Thompson on September 17, 1849. She had saved money by hiring out her labor and had established contacts in the Underground Railroad. The auction block was imminent, she had faith in God, and she yearned for freedom. On October 3, an ad appeared in the *Cambridge Democrat* offering $300 for the capture of the three runaways. Days later, Henry and Benjamin decided it was too much of a risk, especially with Benjamin having recently married and become a father. They decided to turn back, believing they would have a better chance of being sold locally rather than down South. Harriet returned with them but escaped again shortly thereafter, on her own.

Her exact route is not known, but she traveled at night—by the North Star like so many others—to elude slave catchers. A woman, believed to be Quaker, helped on the initial leg of her journey, perhaps northeast along the Choptank River toward Delaware, and directed Harriet to other families that were part of the Underground Railroad. Ironically, one of the stations to which she was directed may have been the home of a Quaker family named Leverton, whose daughter Mary Elizabeth had married a grandson of Anthony Thompson.

Forging into the future by following the North Star

> *"I looked at my hands to see if I was the same person now that I was free. There was such a glory over everything; the sun came like gold through the trees, and over the fields, and I felt like I was in heaven."*
> —HARRIET TUBMAN

With the help of white and black operatives along the clandestine support network on the journey north, Harriet eventually landed in Philadelphia. She was free, but everyone she held dear—her husband, mother, father, brothers, nieces, and nephews—were back in Maryland. True happiness for Tubman would be the ability to share the freedom she was experiencing with the rest of her family. As she later told Bradford,

> *I was free and they should be free. I would make a home in the North and bring them there, God helping me. Oh, how I prayed then.*[4]

Harriet found domestic work in hotels and private homes between Philadelphia and Cape May, New Jersey, all the while planning to return to Maryland to bring back her family. With that mission ever in mind, it would not be long before she met William Still, a leading organizer, conductor, and chronicler of the Underground Railroad, as well as other colleagues of his in the City of Brotherly Love.

Harriet's niece, Kizziah, and her children on the auction block

3

Harriet the Conductor

> *"Great fears were entertained for her safety, but she was wholly devoid of personal fear. The idea of being captured by slave-hunters or slave holders, seemed never to enter her mind."* —WILLIAM STILL

OPPORTUNITY PRESENTED ITSELF IN DECEMBER 1850. Tubman's niece Kizziah and her two children were scheduled to go on the auction block once again. Harriet had kept in touch with events back home through the Underground Railroad network, abolitionists she met in Pennsylvania, family, and friends. With Kizziah's husband John Bowley, she devised a rather risky plan for rescuing her loved ones.

First Rescues

Kizziah and her children, James and Araminta, sold for perhaps $500–$600 and, according to normal practice, were placed in a hold until the buyer could get his money together. This practice gave auctioneers a break and an opportunity to close out the sale following dinner. In the case of Kizziah and her children, however, when the auctioneer returned from dinner, the buyer was nowhere to be found. And when the auctioneer moved to get the three sold slaves out of the hold and back onto the block, they were missing, too!

The Bowley Family escape to a friend's home after the sale.

The highest bidder, it turned out, was Kizziah's husband, John Bowley; because he was a free black man, the sale was perfectly legal (if not entirely acceptable to most whites). And so, while the auctioneer was enjoying his dinner, John whisked off Kizziah, James, and Araminta to a house less than five minutes away, where they found safety. The next night, navigating the treacherous waters of the Chesapeake,

Harriet meets the Bowleys in Baltimore.

John led them to Baltimore—where an anxious Harriet Tubman was awaiting them. She, in turn, escorted them to freedom in Philadelphia. Her grandnephew James became a kind of protégé. She put him through school, and he went on to become a teacher in his own right; after the Civil War, he was elected to the Reconstruction state legislature of South Carolina.

For Tubman, Baltimore became a prime staging ground for leading family members and other slaves to safety and freedom in the North. She plotted and worked there with her brother-in-law, Tom Tubman, who also found her a place to stay. Baltimore's seaport was a perfect location for accessing information about family members in Dorchester County, with less risk of capture.

On the Underground Railroad

The rescue of Kizziah, James, and Araminta in December 1850 was the first of at least thirteen trips that Harriet made back to Maryland, freeing up to seventy slaves in all. (Neither the exact number of missions nor the exact number of people she freed is known for sure, but historical documentation certainly indicates that Sarah Bradford, as well as other biographers and contemporaries, have exaggerated the figures.) Tubman made her second journey south to Baltimore a few months later to help her younger brother, Moses, and two other men find their way to freedom. She continued her exploits until 1860.

While widely acclaimed for her fearlessness and determination in the face of grave dangers, Harriet Tubman did not act in a void. She operated as part of a network of abolitionists, free blacks, and other supporters who worked for the cause of freedom—by sharing information and hiding, transporting, or feeding runaways on the route north—at all costs and at personal risk. This informal network was called the Underground Railroad.

The term "underground railroad" first appeared in a Washington newspaper article in 1839, describing a slave's desire to escape on a metaphorical railroad that "went underground all the way to Boston." Within a few years, the name became synonymous with a clandestine path to freedom on which escaped slaves were called "passengers," those who guided them were called "conductors," and the homes in which they were hidden were called "stations."

The network ran north all the way to Canada, but it was not as extensive or well organized in some areas as in others. The likelihood of escape was more remote in the Deep South, though some resourceful runaways found their way to the Caribbean, South America, and free states and territories in the American West, such as California. The heaviest flow of fugitives originated in the three border states of Maryland, Kentucky, and Virginia meandered north across the Mason-Dixon Line.

Maryland had the largest free black community in the United States as then constituted. Baltimore alone, the "black capital" of the Upper South, had "25,442 men, women, and children in 1850, compared with

FUGITIVE SLAVE LAWS

The Fugitive Slave Act of 1793, passed in the early years of the republic, treated runaway slaves as personal property and gave Southern slaveholders the right to recapture them anywhere in the country (including non-slave states). The problem was that many state laws, and the reluctance of many ordinary citizens to assist, made it difficult for slave owners to reclaim their runaways. The Fugitive Slave Act of 1850, passed as part of the Compromise of 1850 between Northern and Southern states, struck down the efforts of free states to protect accused runaways, imposed fines or imprisonment on ordinary citizens for aiding or assisting a fugitive, and mobilized the army, US marshals, and the federal court system to halt the flight of slaves from the South, capture them in the North, and prosecute officials and citizens who did not turn them in.

As a result of this "Bloodhound Law," as abolitionists dubbed it, slaves who escaped from the South did not find true safety in the so-called free states and set their sights farther north on Canada—the final destination for thousands on the Underground Railroad.

fewer than 3,000 slaves."[1] That fact, combined with its proximity to the North and a well-developed transportation system by train or ship, made it a major hub for operators of the Underground Railroad.

This does not mean that enslaved people escaped only from Maryland and the other border states. They ran off from other locations, too, but often they did not take the route north. Some fugitives from the Deep South would run to New Orleans, Louisiana, or Mobile, Alabama, and try to blend in with the free black populations in those cities. Others escaped to Native American territory, or Mexico, or nearby British possessions like the Bahama Islands.

The informal network of the Underground Railroad, whose activities date to the early 19th century and peaked in the 1850s, assisted in the flight to freedom of the largest number of runaways—as many as 100,000 by the end of the Civil War in 1865—from the Southern states, to the Northern states, and on to Canada. There were no physical trains or tracks to carry the runaways anywhere, and the network was far less organized and reliable in the Deep South than it was in the border states and the North. In many places it did not exist at all. (The Mississippi River Valley was the primary conduit from Louisiana, Mississippi, Arkansas, and Missouri.) Especially in the Deep South, most slaves ran on their own devices. For many, there was no conductor waiting to guide them to freedom and no ready station in which to hide or find passage. The great abolitionist and orator Frederick Douglass, who grew up a slave on Maryland's Eastern Shore, escaped

Frederick Douglass

33

David Ruggles

by hopping a *real* train and never met a conductor of the Underground Railroad until reaching New York. (That conductor was David Ruggles, "a forceful, courageous voice for black freedom" and the founder of an abolitionist group called the New York Committee of Vigilance.[2])

And so, both before and after the Fugitive Slave Act of 1850, the Underground Railroad of clandestine station houses, secret hiding places, and benevolent conductors was far more developed and dependable for fugitive slaves after they made it across the border into a free state. The Quaker abolitionist Levi Coffin, of Indiana and later Ohio, began housing fugitives in 1826—a full twelve years before Frederick Douglass escaped from Maryland. With his wife Catherine, Coffin ushered more than 2,000 former slaves through Newport (now Fountain City), Indiana, and Cincinnati, Ohio. Coffin became known as the unofficial "president of the Underground Railroad" and his home in Newport as its "Grand Central Station."

Levi Coffin

> "The Bible, in bidding us to feed the hungry and clothe the naked, said nothing about color, and I should try to follow out the teachings of that good book."
> —LEVI COFFIN

Across the Ohio River in Cincinnati, a considerable number of free black families and white sympathizers came to the aid of slave families that made the perilous journey from Kentucky and bondage (like Eliza and her son in *Uncle Tom's Cabin*). Especially after the Fugitive Slave Act of 1850, when many runaways were pursued by slave catchers, it was difficult with the means they had to hide and protect themselves. The Underground Railroad provided support with the housing, provisions, wagons, and finances needed to avoid capture and move on to Canada. Levi Coffin set up a store and wholesale warehouse stocked only with goods made by free labor to compete with Southern goods produced by slaves.

Tubman never met Coffin, but she certainly knew Thomas Garrett, another Quaker organizer and a longtime conductor of the Underground Railroad in Pennsylvania and Delaware. Garrett was a key figure on one of the three "liberty lines"—which Tubman frequented heavily in her rescue missions—from Maryland to Pennsylvania. Garrett's network included dependable people and secure waystations between Washington, DC, and Wilmington, Delaware (a slave state). Then it was on to Philadelphia, where William Still and his organization housed the fugitives, recorded their testimonies, and prepared them for their new lives there or in Canada. The stations farther south that Tubman relied on were largely her friends and relatives, mostly free blacks. She would lean on them heavily for communication and shelter in her rescue missions to come.

Thomas Garrett

William Still

35

Missions of Freedom: 1851–1854

It was on Harriet's third trip south—in the fall of 1851, some two years after her own escape—that she risked recapture by venturing beyond Baltimore and slipping back into Dorchester County. This time she was going for her husband, John Tubman. She saved money for the journey, bought him a suit of clothes, and stole south.

Harriet found her husband but was startled—and devastated—to learn that he had taken another wife, named Caroline. John had moved on with his life, said that he was happy where he was, and wanted to stay. Fighting through her anguish and determined that it would not destroy her, Harriet found other family members and, for the first time, unrelated slaves who were eager to escape, and led all eleven of them to safety in Philadelphia.

With the Fugitive Slave Act in full force, escaped slaves no longer felt safe crossing north into Pennsylvania, Ohio, New York, or even Massachusetts, and extended their journeys farther up into Canada. There is no reliable documentation of Tubman's fourth rescue mission in late 1852, and it's possible that some or all of the fugitives may have been Tubman's passengers from a previous journey—in other words, that the fourth mission was actually an extension of the third.

In any event, there is evidence that Tubman and eleven former Maryland slaves stayed over at the home of Frederick Douglass in Rochester, New York, near Lake Ontario and the Canadian border. Douglass describes the incident in one of his autobiographies:

> On one occasion I had eleven fugitives at the same time under my roof, and it was necessary for them to remain with me until I could collect sufficient money to get them to Canada. It was the largest number I ever had at any one time, and I had some difficulty in providing so many with food and shelter, but, as may well be imagined, they were not very fastidious in either direction, and were well content with very plain food, and a strip of carpet on the floor for a bed, or a place on the straw in the barnloft.[3]

The time of the visit and the number of fugitives suggest strongly that it was Tubman and her followers. Tubman and Douglass remained great friends and collaborators in the cause of freedom and abolition.

Douglass and Tubman

One of Harriet's most rewarding rescue missions—her sixth—came on Christmas Day, 1854. This time there were ten passengers on the return trip, including three of her brothers and possibly some of the Bowleys. Harriet's brother Ben was in love with a woman on another farm whose master had refused her permission to marry. And so they had determined to run off together. Ben left a suit of men's clothing for her at a garden hiding place, where the woman found it and exchanged it for her own clothes. Then she let her dress float down the stream and slipped off the farm without detection. She connected with her future husband and Harriet before heading on to Philadelphia and then to Canada.

❖ ❖ ❖

Ben's future wife,
Jane Kane, suits up
for escape.

With each successful mission, her knowledge, connections, and reputation continued to grow. She gained confidence and built her own network of operatives and routes all the way from Maryland to Canada. Collaborators and admirers included the likes of Thomas Garrett, Frederick Douglass, and Stephen Myers and Jermain Wesley Loguen in upstate New York.

The authorities in Maryland, meanwhile, were confounded. Little did they suspect that Minty Tubman, the tiny, frail runaway, was behind the escape of so many slaves. At just five feet tall and still suffering from headaches and fainting spells, she endured great risk and physical exertions. She relied on her religious faith and sheer ingenuity, often donning a disguise to deflect attention. She varied her routes, carried a revolver, and was not afraid to brandish it (though she is not known ever to have fired it).

Still includes Ben and Jane's story as well as those of the rest of Harriet's "cargo run" in his Narratives.

38

Among the other key figures of the Underground Railroad whom Tubman encountered—and became admirers—was William Still of Philadelphia. Aside from being one of the organizers and linchpins of the clandestine antislavery network in that city, Still collected and maintained records, personal accounts, and testimonials of the 649 fugitives he ushered to freedom in Pennsylvania and then Canada. The personal histories, letters, and related documents would later be published as *The Underground Railroad: A Record of Facts, Authentic Letters, &C., Narrating the Hardships, Hair Breadth Escapes, and Death Struggles of the Slaves in their Efforts for Freedom, As Related by Themselves and others or Witnessed by the Author* (1872). It was the most complete firsthand account of the operations of the Underground Railroad.

Harriet Tubman passed through Still's station on several occasions during the 1850s, and her passengers were among those whose stories he collected. They included six fugitives who had fled with her from Dorchester County on Christmas Day, 1854, and arrived at Still's

WILLIAM STILL, the great conductor and historian of the Underground Railroad in Philadelphia, was a free-born black whose parents, Levin and Charity Still, had been slaves on Maryland's Eastern Shore. Levin's master set him free, Charity escaped, and the couple settled in New Jersey. William was their eighteenth child. Two of his brothers, Levin, Jr. and Peter, were sold into slavery in the Deep South as young boys—the story of which motivated William in his work as an abolitionist and rescuer of runaways.

Levin, Jr. died from a whipping, but Peter was finally able to buy his freedom in Alabama at the age of 50. Arriving in Philadelphia, he enlisted the help of the Pennsylvania Anti-Slavery Society to search for his birth parents and siblings. Working as a clerk for the organization in August 1850, William Still listened to the man's story and came to a stunning realization. At first he was speechless. Then he said, "Suppose I should tell you that I am your brother."

The reunion inspired William Still to keep meticulous records on every fugitive slave he encountered.

Philadelphia home on December 29. Two of those passengers were the brothers with whom Harriet had first set out five years before and then turned back—Henry and Benjamin. According to Still's records, Benjamin, now 28, "was the so-called property of Eliza Ann Brodins (Brodess), who lived near Bucktown, in Maryland. Benjamin did not hesitate to say, in unqualified terms, that his mistress was 'very devilish.'"[4] Henry, now 22, "had quite an insight into matters and things going on among slaves and slave-holders generally, in country life. He was the father of two small children, whom he had to leave behind."[5] Also part of the group were Harriet's brother Robert and Ben's fiancée, Jane Kane.

Still's book entry on Tubman's arrival, which begins with a letter from Thomas Garrett about how he met Tubman, describes the diminutive Underground Railroad conductor as the Moses of her people:

> She had faithfully gone down into Egypt, and had delivered these six bondmen by her own heroism. Harriet was a woman of no pretensions, indeed, a more ordinary specimen of humanity could hardly be found among the most unfortunate looking farm hands of the South. Yet, in point of courage, shrewdness and disinterested exertions to rescue her fellowmen, by making personal visits to Maryland among the slaves, she was without her equal.[6]

Later Journeys: 1855–1860

From 1851 to 1857, Tubman made a total of eleven journeys between Maryland and the town of St. Catharines, Canada (just beyond Niagara Falls and the New York State border in Ontario), which became her main residence and base of operations beginning in the summer of 1856. A large community of ex-slaves had gathered in the town following passage of the Fugitive Slave Act of 1850; among them were a number of Harriet's family members and friends. From St. Catharines, Tubman made at least one trip, sometimes two, down into Maryland every year. She usually traveled in wintertime, when daylight hours were short and people tended to stay indoors. She liked to arrange for escapes on Saturday night, so the runaways might not be missed until Monday morning. When in the "Land of Egypt," she stuck to back-roads and traveled under the stars.

One of her riskiest rescue missions came in October 1856, at the request of an escaped slave in St. Catharines who was desperate to be reunited with his fiancée, a young slave woman in Baltimore named Tilly. In the second of her three trips south that year, Tubman obtained a certificate from a Philadelphia steamship captain stating that she was a free resident; with that, she traveled on his ship through the Chesapeake and Delaware Canal to Baltimore. She was able to locate Tilly there, but she would need a $500 bond or a certificate of freedom for the young woman in order to travel safely by boat back to Philadelphia. Instead, Tubman and Tilly were able to obtain the necessary paperwork from a captain in Baltimore who was friends with the one in Philadelphia. They made their way onto a steamer called the *Kent* that carried mail, freight, and passengers south on the Chesapeake to the town of Seaford, Delaware. From there, they were able

Praying for God's continued favor and passage north

to gain passage by train to the town of Camden and then by carriage to Wilmington.

The most harrowing moments of the journey came on Baltimore's Inner Harbor as they awaited the departure of the *Kent*. Harassed on the way to the dock by possible slave catchers, Tubman held up her papers as they moved toward the vessel. The captain had them stand aside and wait for the other passengers to board, which gave Harriet a moment to pray. She once noted that she never went on a journey without God's direction; now she took a moment to let God know that she needed His intervention. *"Oh Lord,"* she prayed, *"you been with me in six troubles, don't desert me in the seventh,"*[7] referencing the six calamities visited upon Job in the Old Testament. As Tilly silently panicked, Harriet repeated the plea. A few moments later, the captain walked over to her, tapped her on the shoulder, and told her they could proceed.

Some historians have inferred from the prayer that Tubman was on her seventh rescue mission, but it seems likely that this was her tenth. Perhaps it was the seventh time that she asked for divine intervention.

That need arose again just weeks later, in mid-November 1856. Tubman was compelled to return to Maryland a number of times for family members, but she never turned away others who made contact. Some did so through her father, Ben Ross, who had been manumitted at age 45 but continued to work as a timber foreman on the Caroline County plantation of Dr. Anthony C. Thompson. A strapping slave named Joe Bailey, recently purchased by a planter named William Hughlett in Talbot County, had approached Ben after being whipped and told him that he and his brother William were ready to run.

On the night of November 15, Harriet Tubman led Joe, his brother William, and two other slaves onto the road to Delaware. The enraged slave owner, who had just paid $2,000 for Joe Bailey, put out a reward of $1,500 and set out in furious pursuit. The 75-mile trip to

Wilmington, which would have normally taken 3–4 days, now took the fugitives nearly two weeks on foot through woods, fields, and swamp. When the group finally arrived in Wilmington, they discovered that their pursuers had arrived three days before and posted reward signs. People in the free black community followed after the slave owners and tore down the notices, but the police were patrolling too tightly for Harriet to follow the regular course to Thomas Garrett's safe house.

In disguise and hiding out with sympathizers, they eluded authorities until Harriet was able to send a message to Garrett. He, in turn, sent a carriage filled with bricks and workers; Harriet and her passengers escaped that night, hidden in the wagon under the hay. From Wilmington, the group made its way to Philadelphia and north into New York—chased every step of the way. Reward posters were everywhere.

Joe fell into deep despair, even as they approached the Canadian border in a railcar. As they crossed the Niagara River Suspension Bridge north of Buffalo, Harriet was eager for her despondent passenger to see the great waterfalls and the final passage to freedom.

"Joe, come look at de Falls! Joe, you fool you, come see de Falls! It's your last chance." But Joe sat still and never raised his head. At length Harriet knew by the rise in the center of the bridge, and the descent on the other side, that they had crossed "the line." She sprang across to Joe's seat, shook him with all her might, and shouted, "Joe, you've shook de lion's paw!" Joe did not know what she meant. "Joe, you're free!" shouted Harriet.

Then Joe's head went up, he raised his hands on high, and his face, streaming with tears, to heaven, and broke out in loud and thrilling tones:

"Glory to God and Jesus too,
One more soul is safe!
Oh, go and carry de news,
One more soul got safe."[8]

None of Tubman's expeditions was more important to her than the one in June 1857, when she finally succeeded in rescuing her aging parents. Ben, who had been able to buy Rit's freedom from Eliza Brodess for $20 two years earlier, was rightly suspected of having aided a number of area slaves in escape—including his sons on Christmas Day, 1854. Ben's reputation with his former owner, Anthony Thompson, and other area whites had kept him above suspicion for a time, but he was known among blacks who yearned for freedom as the person to approach for making arrangements.

Christmas night in the corn shed

So safe and protective of the truth was Ben Ross that, on that Christmas Day, he met up with his sons and daughter Harriet—whom he had not seen in five years—wearing a blindfold. It was important to be able to tell the owner and slave catchers that he had not seen them. Nor did any of them tell Rit before they left, concerned for her safety if she knew anything.

As recounted in Sarah Bradford's *Scenes in the Life of Harriet Tubman*, the posse came looking for the slave brothers after the holiday with the intention of selling them. Not finding any in their cabins, the men went to the "big house" and asked Dr. Thompson if he had seen them. Thompson says he hasn't and asks,

"Have you been down to Old Ben's?"
"Yes."
"What does Old Rit say?"
"Old Rit says not one of 'em came this Christmas. She was looking for 'em most all day, and most broke her heart about it."
"What does Old Ben say?"
"Old Ben says that he hasn't seen one of his children this Christmas."
"Well, if Old Ben says that, they haven't been round."[9]

Ben resumed his activities in the Underground Railroad, and it wasn't long before he was back under suspicion. He sheltered nine runaways in his cabin in March 1857, but one of them turned back and, it appears, turned informant. As authorities were preparing to arrest him, Harriet rushed south to save the couple. It was her only mission known to have taken place in summer, and it put her at particular risk. Her parents' advanced ages posed another challenge, as they were unable to walk long distances. And finally, both had possessions with which they refused to part. For Rit, it was a feather bed; for Ben, it was a prized axe.

Somehow, Harriet was able to load her elderly parents and their possessions onto a wagon and transport them all the way to Wilmington. They arrived at Thomas Garrett's on June 4, and he arranged passage for them to William Still in Philadelphia. Still interviewed Ben and Rit as fugitives from slavery even though they were free. He never mentioned that they were Harriet Tubman's parents; nor did he make any reference to Ben's Underground Railroad activities. Yet Still was quite correct in recognizing the couple as fugitives from the law. Had Ben stayed in Maryland, he would have been arrested the very next day.

Final Expedition

Harriet Tubman's last known rescue mission came in November–December 1860, when she saved seven more slaves from the violence and degradation of bondage. For instead of taking her parents all the way to St. Catharines, where they would settle peacefully, she left them in the care of friends in New York and headed back to the Eastern Shore to retrieve her sister Rachel and Rachel's two children.

Tubman had been aching to save her sister for years. On a prior occasion, the Christmas after her brothers' escape, Brodess had suspended Rachel's visiting privileges and separated her from her children. Harriet was able to help two large groups of slaves make successful escape plans in October 1857, but Rachel remained out of reach; she may have been hired out miles away. The multitude of slaves who had run away that fall created an air of desperation for owners, and the underground network was heavily disrupted; a number of conductors were either jailed or fled the state. Tubman left Maryland without any passengers on that trip in late 1857, and her rescue missions came to a halt.

The sisters were able to regain communication, and Harriet remained determined to go back for her one last time. Rachel thought she might be allowed to be with her children for Christmas, and Harriet planned the journey even though more restrictions had been imposed and many of the people she had long depended on were no longer in place.

Harriet would never see her sister again. For when she arrived back in Dorchester County in December 1860, she learned that Rachel had died. Unable to locate her niece and nephew, Tubman resolved not to make the trip a wasted one again. Instead she brought with her five members of the Ennals family—including an infant child who had to be drugged so her cries would not give them away—and two other slaves. After weeks of traveling, the group arrived safely in St. Catharines, Ontario. Rachel's two children remained in bondage.

Harriet leading the way

The last seven brought the total number of slaves that Tubman personally led to freedom from Dorchester and surrounding areas to at least seventy. Although early biographers and historians exaggerated the figures—some suggested there were hundreds. It is also true that Tubman lent indirect assistance in the form of information, inspiration, and advice to scores of others. The two groups of runaways whose plans she abetted in October 1857 alone—numbering sixteen and twenty-eight, respectively—were referred to in the press as the "Stampede of Slaves."

The total number of slaves that Harriet Tubman saved personally or assisted indirectly thus has been estimated at 120–140. "I was the conductor of the Underground Railroad for eight years," she was later quoted as saying, "and I can say what most conductors can't say—I never ran my train off the track and I never lost a passenger." [10]

As in the rescue of Tilly on the docks of Baltimore, she found her strength in God and His direction.

47

HOW MUCH WAS HARRIET TUBMAN WORTH?

A common myth associated with Harriet Tubman is that there was a $40,000 reward offered for her capture. (In contrast, rewards for individual run-away slaves ranged from approximately $100 to $1,600.) This myth was begun by Sarah Bradford in her 1886 biography, *Harriet Tubman, Moses of Her People*.

This bounty amount is highly improbable, in that for the entire time that she was running her trips back and forth from "Egypt," slavecatchers had not heard of her.

Though the $40,000 figure has been debunked by prominent historians, Tubman's frequency on the abolitionist and women's suffrage speech circuit did gain her enough notoriety in pro-slavery circles to warrant a substantial reward. It is thought that the reward could have been as high as $12,500, but no evidence has been found to substantiate the actual amount.

By 1860, Tubman became a household name in both abolitionist and slave-proponent circles. Proof of her new status was public criticism. John Bell Robinson of Philadelphia was a journalist and slavery advocate. After attending or reading about one of Tubman's speeches at Boston's Melodian Hall in 1860, he wrote: "What could be more insulting after having lost $50,000 worth of property by that deluded negress, than for that large congregation of whites and well educated people of Boston to endorse such an imposition on the Constitutional rights of the slave States?" Robinson went on to decry Tubman's rescue of her parents as parental abuse by claiming they would have been much better left in Maryland, "caressed and better taken care of...sitting in ease around the plentiful board of their master."

Regardless of the amount of the reward, it was clear that the stakes were much higher when she made her last run in 1860. But the history that lay ahead of her would show that her value could not be estimated.

4

A Woman Called Moses and the Black Church's Prophetic Vision

> *"I said to the Lord, 'I'm going to hold steady on to you, and I know you'll see me through.'"*
> —HARRIET TUBMAN

WILLIAM WELLS BROWN, A PROMINENT ABOLITION-ist, author, and former slave, traveled from Boston to Ontario, Canada, in 1860 and inter-viewed some of the friends and family members whom Harriet Tubman had helped flee north over the previous decade. The whites "can't catch Moses," they told Brown, "'cause, you see, she's born with the charm. The Lord has given Moses the power."[1]

The charm was Tubman's unswerv-ing faith in God.

It was a supernatural connec-tion that allowed Tubman to set aside fears of capture and to venture back into what

William Wells Brown

Thomas Wentworth Higgenson

she called "Egypt Land" again and again. If anyone had an excuse to forgo thoughts of rescuing relatives or anyone else, it was Harriet Tubman. The effects of Tubman's childhood head injury, not to mention her repeated rescue missions and sometimes brazen plans, made the likelihood of being caught extremely high. After passage of the Fugitive Slave Act in 1850, slave hunters were prevalent everywhere and the bounties were high. Yet Tubman's contemporaries described her time and again as fearless. "She was apparently proof against all adversaries,"[2] wrote William Still. In an 1859 letter, the Unitarian minister and radical abolitionist Thomas Wentworth Higginson wrote the following about her:

> . . . a more ordinary specimen of humanity could hardly be found among the most unfortunate-looking farm hands of the South. Yet in point of courage, shrewdness, and disinterested exertions to rescue her fellow-man, she was without equal.[3]

Tubman made at least thirteen trips into slave territory and back out to freedom without losing a single follower along the way. Believers in a Supreme Being would view this as testimony to God's devotion to humanity; non-believers would view it as testimony to the power of the human will. Tubman, for her part, had no doubts as to who directed her path: She said she never went on a rescue unless she was directed personally by God.

Wrote Thomas Garrett, the Quaker abolitionist and Underground Railroad organizer:

> *I never met with any person, of any color, who had more confidence in the voice of God, as spoken direct to her soul. She has frequently told me that she talked with God, and He talked with her everyday of her life. . . .*[4]

Biblical Connections

Like her biblical namesake Moses, and the patriarch Abraham before him, Tubman was recognized by many people who knew her, as well as some members of later generations who learned her story, as having a supernatural connection that allowed her to converse with the Almighty. This is not an unusual spiritual idea for, or about, a slave woman. Enslaved Africans saw many similarities between their plight and that of the Jews in the Book of Exodus. In the view of blacks in bondage, the evil Pharaoh and slave overseers who tyrannized the ancient Israelites were akin to the white plantation owners and slave drivers who oppressed them.

And so, in this and other ways, Harriet Tubman's slavery-to-freedom story came to be seen as a 19th-century extension of the stories of the Judeo-Christian Bible. While placing an unshakable faith in God and Jesus, she was recognized for the attributes and abilities of an Old Testament prophet: a lowly but strong-willed person who establishes a direct connection with God through personal salvation and, as a direct result, has visions of the future and performs remarkable feats. Those feats are *powerful, physical manifestations of her faith* that believers in a Supreme Being, then and now, would consider miracles. As in the stories of Old Testament prophets, her divinely guided works allow the people around her to trust in her unconditionally, and she succeeds in transforming society on the strength of her faith.

Home, Church, and Prophecy

Harriet Tubman grew up in a devoutly religious household, where faith in God included acts of devotion. Her father fasted regularly. As Harriet later described it,

> *Going from Good Friday, my father never eats or drinks, all day, fasting for the five bleeding wounds of Jesus. All the other Fridays of the year, he never eats till the sun goes down; then he takes a little tea and a piece of bread. . . . He says if he denies himself for the sufferings of his Lord and Master, Jesus will sustain him.*[5]

Yet the faith of Harriet's family, like that of so many enslaved Africans in America, did not blind them to the levels of hypocrisy practiced by white Christian churches. Blacks, both free and slave, saw a clear distinction between the Christian faith as they practiced it and the Christian faith as whites who had taught it to them practiced it.

Christian churches in the American South during the early to mid-1800s differed by the color of their congregations and by their preachings on race. There were churches for whites, churches for free blacks, churches for slaves created by their masters, and churches—or private services—that slaves held for themselves. All four practiced a form of fundamentalist Christianity in which individual salvation comes only from a hard-won personal relationship with God and strict adherence to agreed-upon doctrine—a belief in the Holy Bible as both God-given scripture and world historical fact. The differentiating factors included teachings about white supremacy and black servitude, slavery and freedom.

White Southern churches, whether middle- or upper-class, preached that whites were blessed by God because they followed His commandments and the teachings of Jesus Christ. White Jesus, they taught, rewarded his faithful servants—slaveholders, their families, and their communities—with material abundance. Their prosperity was ensured by African savages—descendants of the cursed children of Ham of the Old Testament—whom they had brought into the flock.[6] The brand of Christianity as taught by white churches in the Deep South affirmed and rewarded a supremacist caste system that plantation owners constructed to maintain their labor-intensive, cotton-based economy. Wealthy white Christians there thanked God for the color of their skin, their natural preeminence, and the riches they amassed through the blood and sweat of African slaves. (Quakers were one notable exception to any Christian notion of white superiority, opposing slavery from the 18th century on. They placed pressure on anyone, including fellow Quakers, who owned slaves to free them. In Maryland, their push for manumission marked the beginning of the free black society.)

The Christianity of free blacks stressed that God rewards faith and that He would eventually deliver them from bondage, as He did for the Jews in Egypt. It's highly possible that Harriet's family attended outdoor services or heard traveling preachers representing free black churches. The decades leading up to the Civil War saw the emergence of free black women preachers— Zilpha Elaw, Jarena Lee, Sojourner Truth, and others—whose sermons the Rosses may have heard or heard about.

Evangelist Jarena Lee

The church services that owners made their slaves attend, sometimes right on plantation grounds, were designed to keep the slaves grateful, faithful, and docile. Services stressed the doctrine that God and his white son, Jesus, had ordained their role of servitude and that being faithful to their masters—who had saved their heathen souls from African paganism—was a way of showing devotion to God.[7] And so, for instance, Dr. Anthony Thompson, a licensed Methodist minister, felt that he was fulfilling his spiritual and benevolent obligation by insisting that his slaves attend services. Interviewed by William Still in 1857, Ben Ross reported that Pastor Thompson had sold more than one of his slaves to plantation owners in Georgia—making him "a wolf in sheep's clothing."[8]

The church services that enslaved Africans conducted on their own, often in secret, stressed their impending deliverance from bondage and the eternal punishment that God, in Old Testament mode, would visit upon those who perpetuated Pharaoh's evil by enslaving, torturing, and killing blacks. In their eyes, it was they—the slaves—who practiced the *true* Christianity and nurtured a *true* relationship with God. Their brand of Christian faith entailed an abiding belief in emancipation by the same God who liberated the Israelites and the same Jesus who liberated their souls from sin.

And so they believed that it was doing God's work to bring about that liberation. Here was the religion of Harriet Tubman and others who defied the ways of Pharaoh. Here was the religion of radical abolitionists and slave rebellion leaders, such as Nat Turner and Denmark Vesey, who carried out Old Testament–style retribution against white slave owners. And here was the religion of a white abolitionist named John Brown, who would soon meet Tubman and, like her, have a major impact on the institution of slavery and American history in general.

Visions of Freedom

Were they powerful intuitions? Divinely inspired prophecies? Vestiges of her African ancestry? Out-of-body experiences associated with her head injury as a youth? (Historians believe that she had temporal lobe epilepsy, or TLE, a condition that can result in seizures, sleeping spells, and visions.[9]) A combination of all of these?

Thomas Garrett offers an example of Tubman's intuition that he finds "unexplainable":

> *In one instance, when she had two stout men with her . . . God told her to stop, which she did; and then asked him what she must do. He told her to leave the road, and turn to the left; she obeyed, and soon came to a small stream of tide water; there was no boat, no bridge. She again inquired of her Guide what she was to do. She was told to go through. It was cold, in the month of March; but having confidence in her Guide, she went in; the water came up to her arm-pits; the men refused to follow till they saw her safe on the opposite shore. They then followed, and if I mistake not, she had soon to wade a second stream; soon after which came to a cabin of colored people, who took them all in, put them to bed and dried their clothes, ready to proceed next night on their journey.*[10]

They found out later that the owners of the slaves who were with her had been at the railroad station near where she had turned off, putting up posters offering a large reward for their capture. Had Tubman and the men continued on that road, they would have been caught.

As a child, Minty Ross was told that she was of Ashanti lineage—descended from a great people and culture in West Africa (present-day Ghana). She had no way of knowing for sure, and there is no historical evidence to confirm or deny the assertion. But there is one hint . . .

Before gaining her own freedom, Harriet had recurring dreams of flying like a bird over fields, towns, and even mountains. At last she would reach a great fence or river. "But," she reported, "it would appear that I wouldn't have the strength and just as I was sinking down, there would be ladies all dressed in white and they would put out their arms and pull me in."[12] The dream of escape was constant for her, to be sure, and "when she came North she remembered these very places as those she had seen in her dreams."[11] This particular ending triggered Harriet's expectation that people would be waiting for her when she finally made it to Philadelphia.

The 20th-century British anthropologist Robert Rattray, who studied dreaming among the Ashanti, made two relevant observations: first, that dream travels were real events for the Ashanti, and second, that dreams of flying were common for them. "If you dream that you have been carried up to the sky . . . and that you have returned to the ground . . . means long life," he wrote.[13] Harriet would live to be 91.

The visions seemed to run in her family, and they were not about insubstantial topics. According to Tubman, her father (descended from the Ashanti or not) had the same gift. Ben, she maintained, predicted the coming of the Mexican–American War.[14] In 1860, Tubman herself predicted the freedom of her people a full three years before the Emancipation Proclamation. According to Sarah Bradford, Harriet was visiting the prominent black abolitionist Henry Highland Garnet and his family in New York when a vision came to her in the night:

> She rose singing, "My people are free! My people are free!" She came down to breakfast singing the words in a sort of ecstasy. She could not eat. The dream or vision filled her whole soul, and physical needs were forgotten. Mr. Garnet said to her: "Oh, Harriet! Harriet! You've come to torment us before the time; do cease this noise! My grandchildren may see the day of the emancipation of our people, but you and I will never see it."
>
> "I tell you, sir, you'll see it, and you'll see it soon. My people are free! My people are free."
>
> Three years later, President Lincoln's proclamation was signed and while everyone was rejoicing, Tubman was quiet.
>
> Someone asked, "Why do you not join with the rest in their rejoicing!"
>
> "Oh," she answered, "I had my jubilee three years ago. I rejoiced all I could then; I can't rejoice no more."[15]

As traditionally celebrated in classrooms and standard texts, Harriet Tubman is a figure of historical significance because she embodies the American values of faith in God and triumph over adversity. Her story is that of a 19th-century woman, born into slavery, who was committed to freedom and equality—democratic concepts, given by God, to which she devoted her life. Moreover, according to this narrative, her freedom and the hard-won freedom of her people is both a human right and a distinctly American manifestation of personal responsibility, which includes establishing a personal relationship with God. That narrative and those values would be welcome in any 21st-century white American church.

But to the oppressed in America and around the world who personally identify with her, the story of Harriet Tubman is a continuation and affirmation of truths found in the Holy Bible rather than in history books. To them, Tubman's narrative offers *religiously and historically undeniable* testimony that God is ever and always on the side of the downtrodden and despised. The facts of her life show that God will continue to create liberators who will destroy the walls of any Jericho if they are faithful to Him and the righteousness of His cause. That level of faith and commitment allows God to give men and women of unyielding faith and strength of will, like Harriet, the power to create miracles that others cannot duplicate. Those miracles symbolically split the history of the world in the same way that Moses, using the power of God, literally parted the Red Sea in the Book of Exodus. And *that* story—*that* truth—would be welcome in any 21st-century black American church.

> *"God's time is always near. He set the North Star in the heavens; He gave me the strength in my limbs; He meant I should be free."* —HARRIET TUBMAN

~ 5 ~

John Brown and the Missed Appointment

> *"The first I see is General Tubman, the second is General Tubman, and the third is General Tubman."*
> —JOHN BROWN, shaking hands three times with Harriet Tubman upon meeting

A T THE NATIONAL LEVEL, PASSAGE OF THE KANSAS–Nebraska Act of 1854 inflamed the longstanding sectional dispute over slavery and radicalized some members of the antislavery movement. Notable among those was John Brown, an abolitionist from New England and upstate New York who resettled in the Kansas Territory. Overturning the Missouri Compromise of 1820, the Kansas–Nebraska Act ignited the power struggle over the nation's westward expansion by declaring that the new territories of Kansas and Nebraska would decide for themselves whether or not to permit slavery (a doctrine known as "popular sovereignty").

The Missouri Compromise had established the 36° 30' parallel as a frontier boundary that outlawed slavery to the north and allowed it to the south. Until then, the country was evenly divided between free states and slave states—eleven each. Missouri's proposed entry into the Union created a controversy that the 1820 compromise appeared to solve. Congress agreed that Missouri would be admitted as a slave state, Maine would be admitted as a free state, and the status of any new states would be determined by their location above or below the 36° 30' parallel. Abolitionists continued to resist the "peculiar institution" and to help runaway slaves, but the Missouri Compromise quelled the immediate political debate and postponed civil war.

Skeptics like Thomas Jefferson, who viewed the Missouri Compromise as "a reprieve only, not a final sentence,"[1] were right in the end. The Kansas–Nebraska Act of 1854 effectively repealed the Missouri Compromise, erased the 36° 30' parallel as a political dividing line, and allowed slavery in any new state if a majority of the population there voted for it. This new legislation outraged opponents of slavery and created activists out of those formerly on the fence. William Cullen Bryant, journalist and editor for *The New York Evening Post*, wrote:

> *If this paper was three times its present size, and if it were issued three times its present size, and if it were issued three times a day instead of once, we could not then have space enough to record the action of patriotic meetings throughout the Northern States protesting against the repeal of the Missouri Compromise by the passage of the Kansas-Nebraska Bill.*[2]

In the newly created Kansas Territory, passage of the bill in May 1854 triggered a battle for popular sovereignty that grew fierce. In the race to see who could gain a majority on the issue, it was slaveholders versus people who were willing to uproot their families for the cause of freedom. Antislavery "Free Staters," some financed by Northeastern business interests, poured into Kansas; proslavery militants referred to as "Border Ruffians" arrived from Missouri and other Southern states. Most of the freesoilers saw an opportunity to win the day through the ballot box. It is not likely that they anticipated the level of resistance and violence they would face. The clash, increasingly violent on both sides, became a virtual guerrilla war known as Bleeding Kansas.

Old John Brown and the Battle for Kansas

The son of a tanner, John Brown was born in 1800 in Torrington, Connecticut, and spent much of his youth in Ohio. He was raised to believe in the Bible and to hate slavery. At age 16, he left home for Massachusetts, where he hoped to become a Congregationalist minister. But eye problems and a lack of money forced him back to his father's tannery and eventually to Pennsylvania, where he married, began a family, and built a business in tanning, leather production, and cattle.

In 1837, now widowed, remarried, and living in Ohio, Brown dedicated himself to the destruction of slavery after the murder of abolitionist newspaper publisher Elijah Parish Lovejoy at the hands of a proslavery mob in Alton, Illinois.

In the years that followed, through the ups and downs of his business ventures (mostly downs), he became active in the antislavery movement and the Underground Railroad in Akron, Ohio, in Springfield, Massachusetts, and at a freedman's community in North Elba, New York. Passage of the Fugitive Slave Act of 1850 and the Kansas–Nebraska Act of 1854 moved him to radicalism. He came to believe that God had chosen him to lead the slaves to freedom.

In 1855, hearing from his adult sons in Kansas that

John Brown

61

the Border Ruffians were running rampant, Brown set out for the territory to take them on. In response to the burning and pillaging of the antislavery town of Lawrence the next spring, Brown and a band of abolitionist settlers, including four of his sons, raided a proslavery settlement at Pottawatomie Creek on the night of May 24. They dragged five settlers from their homes and hacked them to death.

The Pottawatomie Massacre touched off a back-and-forth succession of raids that lasted three months and killed twenty-nine people. The territory and its guerrilla warfare became known as Bleeding Kansas, and John Brown, who had lost three sons, became notorious as a Christian warrior against slavery. With a break in the hostilities that fall, Brown and several surviving sons returned east to raise money from abolitionist supporters. It was time, he believed, to "carry this war into Africa"[3]—his way of saying he would move the fight into the South.

The Calling of Harpers Ferry and Harriet Tubman

Believing that he was called upon by God and that any means were justified to end slavery, Brown spent the next two-and-a-half years raising money in New England to bring his war south. A group of influential abolitionists—later dubbed the "Secret Six"—stepped up to fund the campaign. The plan was to raid the federal arsenal at Harpers Ferry, Virginia (now West Virginia), and use the weapons to trigger a series of armed slave revolts across the South. With the funding in place, Brown began planning the details and making arrangements. Abolitionist leaders such as Frederick Douglass and William Lloyd Garrison either did not endorse his violent tactics or did not believe he would succeed, but Brown ventured to St. Catharines, Ontario, to meet someone he prayed would help with the uprising.

In April 1858, Harriet Tubman and John Brown met for the first time at her home in St. Catharines. From the start, the admiration was mutual. Like Brown, Tubman had heard God's voice calling to her

JOHN BROWN AND THE SECRET SIX

Samuel Gridley Howe
1801–1876

Thomas Wentworth
Higginson
1823–1911

Theodore Parker
1810–1860

John Brown

Franklin Benjamin Sanborn
1831–1917

George Luther Stearns
1809–1874

Gerrit Smith
(1797–1874)

THE SECRET SIX

The Secret Six was a group of New England-based financers formed early in 1858 for the purpose of supporting John Brown's Harpers Ferry raid. The members prepared the minds of the American people for the possibility of war solving the slavery question. They were staunch supporters, but just like any business partners, they wanted their investment to have a real possibility of success. When it appeared that John Brown's hired military trainer, Hugh Forbes, had leaked information about the Harpers Ferry plan to US Senator Hugh Wilson of Massachusetts, the Secret Six quickly became the silent six, withdrawing support for a time. However, after Brown's successful Missouri raid in December 1858, freeing eleven enslaved people, Brown's Secret Six was convinced to recommit to Brown's raid.

Most intriguing about the members was their societal prominence. Four of the members were Harvard graduates—Franklin Benjamin Sanborn, Theodore Parker, Thomas Wenthworth-Higgenson and Samuel Gridley-Howe.

Higgenson was a militant Unitarian minister who would later became a colonel in the Civil War. He would command the 1st South Carolina Volunteers, the first federally authorized black regiment.

Theodore Parker, Higgenson's mentor, was a Transcendentalist and minister of the radical persuasion. His oratory skill would inspire Abraham Lincoln and the Rev. Dr. Martin Luther King.

Samuel Gridley-Howe, whose grandfather was involved in the Boston Tea Party, was a physician who would pioneer in treatment and education of the blind, deaf, and disabled. His wife, Julia Ward Howe, wrote the John Brown tribute "Battle Hymn of the Republic."

Franklin Benjamin Sanborn and Gerrit Smith were early friends of Brown and were likely the first to know about the Harpers Ferry plot. Sanborn, the youngest of the six, was a writer, journalist, and philanthropist. He was the first to write a biographical outline on Harriet Tubman in a Commonwealth article in 1863.

Gerrit Smith, the oldest and known to be the least secret of the six, was a reformer, politician, and philanthropist. He knew Tubman well and his Peterboro mansion was an important station on the Underground.

George Luther Stearns was the successful manufacturer of linseed oil and lead pipe. He was likely the group's wealthiest member. He provided John Brown a couple hundred revolvers and pledged thousands of dollars.

What bonded these six men in such a way as to risk their status, reputation, and even life to take such drastic action? Perhaps the answer can be found in a familiar sounding quote from Theodore Parker while urging his congregation to defy the Fugitive Slave Act of 1850. "What I call the American idea" as "a democracy, that is a government of all the people, by all of the people and for all the people."

directly; indeed she had had a vision of meeting the fiery abolitionist in advance of his arrival. Brown, impressed from the outset by her leadership, courage, and savvy, addressed her as "General Tubman" and routinely referred to her in the masculine. "He is the most of a man, naturally, that I have ever met with," he wrote.[4]

Tubman had never advocated violence against whites as the path to freedom, but she had come to believe that the institution of slavery would only be dissolved in blood. She certainly shared John Brown's fervor for the cause. For him, Tubman's knowledge of local geography and antislavery networks in the border states of Pennsylvania and Maryland were invaluable to the Harpers Ferry mission. So, too, were her connections in the freed black community. After reviewing the plans, Tubman began recruiting among the former slaves in southern Ontario.

Captain Brown meets General Moses

Enlisting volunteers for the mission was not as easy as might have been thought. Many in the black community had just arrived after a treacherous journey from the South, and going back could hardly have been appealing. Canada meant freedom, and though the environment was harsh in the winter months, work was readily available. Some of the men were likely skeptical of leaving their families to follow a white man whose sanity may have been in question. Finally, in the back of everyone's mind, had to be accounts of the slave revolt nearly thirty years before, in August 1831, led by Nat Turner in Southampton County, Virginia. More than sixty slave owners and their families had been killed in that incident, but the rebellion ended with the hanging of all blacks who had participated and the killing of more than a hundred more enslaved men, women, and children. Even closer to home was the 1845 insurrection of approximately seventy-five of Southern Maryland's enslaved lead by Mark Caesar, a free black and carpenter and William Wheeler, a slave. As they set out on July 7th, they didn't set out to kill anyone unless they got in the way of their reaching their destination. It was a march to freedom in broad daylight. They were armed with a pistol, scythe blades, clubs, bludgeons, swords, and clubs. They were surrounded by a militia within two miles of Rockville. Caesar and Wheeler gave the charge to fight back and they did. Many were killed, captured, and sold further south. A few escaped. Wheeler and Caesar were tried and convicted. After four months in a county jail, Wheeler escaped. A bounty of $100 was placed on him. Caesar died in prison of tuberculosis in 1850.

It was clear to many, as it had been to Frederick Douglass and others petitioned to join the campaign, that following John Brown to Harpers Ferry would not end well or spawn the revolution he envisioned. Harriet Tubman, for her part, became a devoted supporter and confidante. She was able to secure dozens of recruits for the Harpers Ferry raid and aided in the planning. What further participation she intended remains open to speculation.

Plans Gone Awry

On May 8, 1858, Brown laid out his plans to several dozen freed blacks and white men at a secret gathering in Ontario. He also presented a "provisional constitution" for governing the region where the slave revolt took hold; the Ontario group agreed to his blueprint and began preparing for the assault that summer. The uprising, according to Brown's plan, would proceed in two major phases: 1) raiding the arsenal at Harpers Ferry, which would provide massive arms and would alert both slaves in the South and abolitionists in the North that a major revolt was underway; and 2) regrouping the original brigade, raiding nearby plantations to free more slaves, and building a guerrilla campaign that would spread south along the Allegheny Mountains.

The momentum came to an abrupt halt, however, when it was learned that one of Brown's key recruits—a former British soldier named Hugh Forbes—may have leaked the plan to a US senator. According to historian Tony Horwitz, Forbes was a disgruntled drillmaster who resorted to blackmail for money he claimed Brown had promised him.[5] Forbes's apparent revelation scared off the Secret Six, forcing Brown to postpone his campaign and return to the Midwest to dispel the leak. Brown continued to refine his plan and solicit support, but confidence in his uprising and the size of his company both diminished.

Unswerving in his devotion to the cause, Brown regained the support of his financers with the rescue of eleven slaves from farms in Missouri. Leading a raid there in December 1858, he took two white hostages and made off with oxen, horses, wagons, and other materials before crossing back into Kansas. Getting the

William H. Seward

eleven fugitive slaves safely to Canada, with a posse and federal marshals in hot pursuit, restored Brown's reputation among abolitionists
and renewed the faith of the Secret Six.

Tubman, for her part, returned the next spring to Auburn, New
York, where she relocated her parents from the bitter Canadian cold in a
house purchased from US Senator William H. Seward. Funds she had
raised in Boston enabled her to make payment on the home and to resume
her "missionary" work—gathering recruits among the young abolitionists, both white and black, that were swarming into Massachusetts.

Harriet's trips back and forth between New England and Auburn
may have hurt her connections among the fugitives in Canada who had
signed up with Brown the previous year. Perhaps they thought the raid
was abandoned, or perhaps they lost faith in the plan. In any event,
Brown was suffering from a lack of support. He rented a farmhouse in
Maryland not far from Harpers Ferry, but only a trickle of recruits
showed up. And it was about this time that his general, Harriet Tubman, fell ill in New York, perhaps related to her childhood head injury.
Historian and biographer Earl Conrad gave this account:

> *Overexertion in her abolition labors, the years of toil on the Under-
> ground Railroad, and the intervals of hard domestic labor to maintain
> herself and her parents had struck Harriet. . . . Her weakness was in a
> stage of general crisis; she was seriously weakened and abed.*[6]

According to most biographers, Harriet had been determined to
meet Brown despite her illness and had started the trek south. Brown
needed her help more than ever, but he was unable to reach her. According to other historians, Tubman was back in Ontario lining up more
recruits. Kate Larson suggests that Tubman may have been in Maryland seeking support for the raid or attempting to free more slaves, or
perhaps that even she doubted Brown's plan at this point. Whatever
the reason, Tubman was not present on the night of October 16, 1859,
when John Brown launched his historic raid on Harpers Ferry.

With a party of just twenty-one men (sixteen white and five black), Brown succeeded in capturing the federal arsenal but was overwhelmed by local militia and a company of US Marines (led by Colonel Robert E. Lee) on the morning of October 18. Brown was captured, tried and convicted of treason, and hanged before year's end.

Despite the failure of his mission, John Brown's passionate opposition to slavery fired the abolitionist cause and left a deep impression on Tubman for the rest of her life. While many would credit Abraham Lincoln for the emancipation of slaves, Tubman would remind listeners of Old John Brown, calling him the white man that blacks should, and would, remember forever. "He done more in dying," she told a friend, "than 100 would in living."[7]

~~ 6 ~~

Nurse, Cook, Soldier, Spy: Harriet's Many Hats in the Civil War

> *"There is a general feeling amongst us that the control of events has been taken out of our hands, that we have fallen into the mighty current of eternal principles [and] invisible force, which are shaping and fashioning events as they wish, using us only as instruments to work out their own results in our National destiny."*
>
> —FREDERICK DOUGLASS[1]

HE LITTLE BONNET IN THE WINDOW WAS ALL THAT the throng of hundreds could see from the street outside. Harriet had made herself unrecognizable by transforming her body and face into those of an old woman, waiting for just the right moment to shed her disguise and alert the crowd.

It was April 27, 1860, in Troy, New York. For Harriet and the abolitionists, here was one more test of the Fugitive Slave Act and the people's resistance to it. The person, or property, in question this time was Charles Nalle, a fugitive slave from Virginia. Nalle had made his escape in October 1858 and was living with the family of a grocer in Troy named William Henry. On that April morning, on his way to the bakery, Nalle was apprehended by a US marshal and a slave catcher working for his former owner. Under the Fugitive Slave Act, Nalle was taken to the US Commissioner's office to be processed for return to Virginia.

Tubman placed a bonnet on Nalle so he could not be easily identified as he was dragged to the river.

Tubman, visiting relatives on her way to Boston, rushed to the site and joined the local sympathizers with her trademark boldness and ingenuity. Disguised as an old woman, she made her way into the building and upstairs where Nalle was being held. As long as her bonnet was visible, the crowd knew that Nalle was still there. When finally the prisoner was being led away, Tubman threw open a window and shouted down, "Here he comes! Take him!" The crowd outside surged around the men exiting the building. Tubman caught up from behind, grabbed hold of Nalle, and covered his head with the bonnet. Pummeled by police and adversaries in the mob, she exhorted the rescuers. "This man shall not go back to slavery! Take him, friends! Drag him to the river! Drown him! But don't let them take him back!"[2]

Spirited through the streets and down to the Hudson River, Nalle gained his freedom a few days later in the nearby town of Watervliet. The rescue, a collective effort by black and white citizens, made national news and was celebrated by abolitionists across the North. Tubman was a hero to the movement once again, but newspapers gave the greatest credit to "rank and file" blacks, or what the *New York Times* called "African fury."[3]

Back Roads to War

If John Brown's raid was the match that lit the fuse of civil war, Charles Nalle's rescue was one of many sparks that signaled change was imminent and would, indeed, be soaked in blood. The first exchange of cannon fire at Fort Sumter was less than a year away, and Harriet Tubman's feats had proven what Brown and others already knew: she had the spirit of a general and, as her bloodied, battered body proved, she could handle a good fight.

Harriet spoke before various antislavery groups through the summer of 1860 and at a women's suffrage gathering on July 4, where she gained notice from a proslavery writer from Philadelphia named John Bell Robinson. He was horrified, Robinson told readers, that a female conductor of the Underground Railroad was being applauded for taking her parents "away from ease and comfortable homes," where they had been "caressed and better taken care of . . . around the plentiful board of their master."[4]

It had been nearly three years since Tubman succeeded in rescuing her parents, not to mention so many others before and after them. She was no longer unknown to authorities—far from it. Tubman had gained a national reputation, which made her expeditions back to Maryland ever riskier. The very last of them, to rescue her sister Rachel and Rachel's two children in November–December 1860 (see Chapter 3), was the most perilous and most disappointing of all. Rachel had died and the children were nowhere to be found. Harriet, determined to make the trip worthwhile, led seven other slaves to freedom, but that journey north took longer than any of the others. The clandestine network on which she had relied for so long was beginning to break down. She would be forced soon to retire from her activity on the Underground Railroad, and political circumstances would lead her back to Canada.

Swearing in a new president of the US during
a time of grave uncertainty

Abraham Lincoln was elected president in November 1860, making civil war seem likely. By the time he was inaugurated early the following March, seven Southern states—South Carolina, Mississippi, Florida, Alabama, Georgia, Louisiana, and Texas—had seceded from the Union. William H. Seward, an active abolitionist and close friend and supporter of Tubman, became Lincoln's secretary of state and was making concessions to keep other Southern states from seceding. Although the effort would prove unsuccessful, his offers of compromise greatly weakened Seward's integrity in the eyes of abolitionists and made Tubman feel at risk. Abolitionist forces already had a wary eye on Seward for his remarks about John Brown and the raid on Harpers Ferry; Seward denounced the attack as "sedition and treason" and expressed his wish that the end of slavery would be "peaceful, voluntary and evolutionary."[5]

All things considered, Harriet felt Canada was the best place for her as the government in Washington tried to appease the Confederacy and avert war. This was no time to test the allegiance of even a friend like Seward, lest he consider giving her up as conciliation to the South. In any event, her days as a conductor on the Underground Railroad were over and new opportunities in the cause of freedom were about to open up.

Aiding Contrabands and Fighting the Snake

The outbreak of fighting between the Union and Confederacy in April 1861, which seems inevitable looking back, abruptly altered the efforts of all those—black and white—who had worked for the cause of abolition and for the freedom and safety of men, women, and children in bondage. The campaigns against slavery out on the frontier, in the halls of government, and along the Underground Railroad gave way to full-fledged war. A Union victory was now the key to abolition even if ending slavery was not President Lincoln's primary reason for fighting. Frederick Douglass, William Wells Brown, and other black leaders were outspoken in calling for the participation of African American troops, but that would not come for more than two years.

For Harriet Tubman, there was no waiting. Like her rescue missions on the Underground Railroad, her role would remain unofficial, behind the scenes, and in the service of runaway slaves. Now, however, she would come to the aid of slave families—a trickle, then a flow, then a flood—that had escaped or been rendered homeless by the fighting and were finding their way north as refugees.

Harriet was back in New England in November 1861 when she heard of the fall of Port Royal, in coastal South Carolina, to Union forces. She immediately began making plans to head south to be of service to newly freed slaves who had made their way to that area. Abolitionist groups got busy raising funds and recruiting teachers, nurses, and other volunteers to work in the encampments. An article in the antislavery newspaper *The Liberator* tells of a fund-raising lecture given by Harriet Tubman at Boston's Twelfth Baptist Church in February 1862.[6] After a trip to upstate New York to make sure her parents were cared for and to say goodbye to her Auburn friends, Harriet set out for Beaufort, South Carolina, by special government transport.

Upon arriving, she reported to General David Hunter, who promptly issued her a free pass throughout the district. A passionate abolitionist, General Hunter was well ahead of President Lincoln in his belief that black men should be armed and allowed to fight in the Union army. Not only did he begin enlisting black soldiers from the occupied districts of South Carolina, but, in May 1862, he issued his own proclamation of freedom for all enslaved people in South Carolina, Florida, and Georgia. His General Order No. 11 began by declaring the three states under martial law and went on as follows:

Slavery and martial law in a free country are altogether incompatible; the persons in these three States—Georgia, Florida, and South Carolina—heretofore held as slaves, are therefore declared forever free.[7]

The president, outraged at Hunter's unauthorized initiative, immediately rescinded the order.

I, Abraham Lincoln, President of the United States, proclaim and declare, that the government of the United States, had no knowledge, information, or belief, of an intention on the part of General Hunter to issue such a proclamation; nor has it yet, any authentic information that the document is genuine— And further, that neither General Hunter, nor any other commander, or person, has been authorized by the Government of the United States, to make proclamations declaring the slaves of any State free; and that the supposed proclamation, now in question, whether genuine or false, is altogether void, so far as respects such declaration.[8]

Hunter continued with his plan of enlisting black soldiers in the 1st South Carolina Volunteers—the first all-black regiment in the army, though it was still unauthorized. Tubman, who greatly respected Hunter for his efforts on behalf of blacks, acted as an intermediary between white soldiers and the contrabands who took up arms. There was a clear distrust of white enlisted men and officers among the black soldiers of the 1st South Carolina, who received no uniforms, weapons, equipment, or even tools for labor from the War Department.

Much of Tubman's work at Port Royal centered on caring for wounded and sick soldiers and the fugitive slaves pouring into the freedman's hospital. Disease was rampant. Using local roots and herbs to brew medicinal tea, Harriet became legendary among the soldiers and contrabands for her healing powers. The need for a strong cure was much on her mind when she dictated a letter to abolitionist Lydia Maria Child about President Lincoln's reluctance to abolish slavery and arm blacks. She was critical of the president and insistent about what he should do.

> *Master Lincoln, he's a great man, and I am a poor negro; but the negro can tell master Lincoln how to save the money and the young men. He can do it by setting the negro free. Suppose that was an awful big snake down there, on the floor. He bite you. Folks all scared, because you die. You send for a doctor to cut the bite; but the snake, he rolled up there, and while the doctor doing it, he bite you again. The doctor dug out that bite; but while the doctor doing it, the snake, he spring up and bite you again; so he keep doing it, till you kill him. That's what master Lincoln ought to know.*[9]

Harriet is making the most of desperate conditions.

Nurse Extraordinaire

It would take Lincoln until July 1862 to draft a proclamation emancipating the slaves in the Confederate states. He issued the executive order in September, and it would take effect on January 1, 1863.

Although the Emancipation Proclamation authorized paid military service by blacks for the first time, Secretary of War Edwin Stanton had commissioned General Rufus Saxton to raise five regiments of black troops in late August 1862. The first one to be federally authorized, following the emancipation in January 1863, was the 1st South Carolina Volunteers. Leading the unit was Tubman's old friend from Boston—and one of the Secret Six financers of the John Brown raid—Colonel Thomas Wentworth Higginson. (The famous 54th Massachusetts Infantry, portrayed in the 1989 film Glory, was authorized two months later and made up of free Northern blacks.)

54th Massachusetts- Ready to win the war.

By the spring of 1863, Harriet had been serving for nearly a year as a mediator between black and white troops and as a nurse at Port Royal, tending to ailing soldiers and civilians. Many were sick and dying of dysentery, typhoid, cholera, malaria, smallpox, and other diseases. The main culprits were water and food contamination, mosquitoes, poor sanitation, and bad hygiene. Malnutrition played a part as well, as many fugitive blacks who entered Union camps had been hiding in the swamps for months. Tubman later described her daily routine and the unsanitary conditions at the hospital.

I'd go to the hospital early every morning. I'd get a big chunk of ice and put it in a basin, and fill it with water; then I'd take a sponge and begin. First man I'd come to, I'd thrash away the flies, and they'd rise, like bees around a hive. Then I'd begin to bathe their wounds, and by the time I'd bathed off three or four, the fire and heat would have melted the ice and made the water warm, and it would be as red as clear blood. Then I'd go and get more ice, and by the time I got to the next one, the flies would be around the first ones, black and thick as ever.[10]

From the very beginning, Tubman had been granted the same rations as the soldiers and officers at Beaufort/Port Royal. But she began to sense the wariness of other freed blacks, who observed the respect she was accorded by foot soldiers and officers alike—right up to Colonel Higginson—who knew her as Black Moses. And so, to forge closer ties with the local people, Harriet gave up her right to full rations and reached out with provisions she prepared herself. Ever resourceful, she would spend her evenings making fifty pies, gingerbread cakes, and casks of root beer. Then, while tending the sick during the day, she would hire contrabands to sell the refreshments at a modest price in local camps. In addition, with $200 she received from the government—the only remuneration she ever received for her service—Harriet opened a wash house and devoted a portion of her time to teaching freedwomen to do laundry as a means of support.

Spy and Scout

The arrival of Colonel James Montgomery during the spring of 1863 was a turning point for the Union campaign in South Carolina, for the black soldiers there, and for the role of Harriet Tubman. Montgomery was assigned the task of raising and commanding a second black regiment in the state. A former ally of John Brown in Bleeding Kansas, Montgomery was well acquainted with—and notorious for—the

Colonel Montgomery followed the intelligence that Harriet
and her spy team gathered, leading to victory.

tactics of guerrilla warfare. He had likely heard of Tubman from John
Brown, which created a bond between them from the start. Mont-
gomery brought his irregular brand of warfare to South Carolina, and
Tubman would play a key role—first as a spy and scout.

Tubman already had been receiving valuable information from
the local black population, which she forwarded to the Union high
command. The locals may not have been aware of her reputation as
Moses, but they witnessed the hard work and sacrifice she made every
day and came to trust her. The intelligence they furnished proved
that Tubman could be an asset in the field, and her partnership with
Montgomery took her directly into some of the most horrific fighting
in the South.

According to later government documents, Tubman rendered "valuable service acting as a spy within the enemies lines—and obtaining the services of the most-valued Scouts and Pilots in the Gov't employ in [the area]."[11] As a spy in her own right, according to General Rufus Saxton, she "made many a raid into enemy lines, displaying remarkable courage, zeal and fidelity."[12] In addition, she recruited and directed the operations of nine men who served as scouts and river pilots. A requisition of $100 in "secret service money" allowed for basic provisions and bribe money for nervous informants still living in Confederate territory. It was likely those informants who provided information about the location of Confederate torpedoes and storage warehouses along the Combahee River north of Beaufort.

The Combahee River Raid

The wartime operation for which Harriet Tubman would be most remembered is one that ran the course of the Combahee River in June 1863. The military goal was to remove Confederate torpedoes and other munitions stored there and to cut off supply lines by destroying bridges and railroad tracks. But the raid was planned and executed primarily as a liberation mission for plantation slaves along the waterway. Tubman may not have commanded the raid, as one newspaper reported, but she played a decisive role in initiating, planning, and executing it. Colonel Montgomery directed the operation, with Tubman at his side.

On June 2, three steam-powered gunboats—the *Sentinel, John Adams,* and *Harriet A. Weed*—set out with 300 men of the 2nd South Carolina Infantry on board. One of Tubman's scouts guided the vessels around mines planted in the river. Once on shore, the Union forces seized large stockpiles of Confederate munitions, supplies, and food. What they could not take with them, they destroyed, setting fire to homes, plantations, storage facilities, machinery, and infrastructure encountered on the way.

Crippling the Confederacy

Montgomery ordered the sounding of steamboat whistles, which signaled to the slaves on shore that it was safe to leave. Hundreds rushed toward the riverbank with their children and scant belongings in tow—chickens, pigs, pots, pans, blankets, and bushels. "I never saw such a sight,"[13] Tubman later reported. The whips, pistols, and threats of their masters posed little threat, though the mission was not without fatalities. Some of the enslaved were killed by rebel soldiers as they fled to the boats.

Converted Ferry Boat poised for battle up the Combahee

All told, more than 750 slaves were freed in the Combahee River raid. "Most of the able bodied men," Harriet later reported, "joined the colored regiments here."[14]

General Hunter was so pleased that he planned to continue this type of operation in other locations. What better way to weaken the enemy than to rob them of their most valuable assets and swell those of the Union! A reporter for the *Wisconsin State Journal* summed up the success of the operation:

Col. Montgomery and his gallant band of 300 Black soldiers under the guidance of a Black woman, dashed into the enemies' country, struck a bold and effective blow, destroying millions of dollars worth of commissary stores, cotton, and lordly dwellings, and striking terror to the heart of rebellion, brought off near 800 slaves and thousands of dollars worth of property, without losing a man or receiving a scratch! It was a glorious consummation.[15]

The reporter singled out Tubman for her "patriotism, sagacity, energy, ability, and all that elevates human character."[16]

In the Fray

The hundreds of refugees who had made their way to Union encampments in the area knew life only through the dark prism of bondage. They were more than ready for a new beginning, hungry for freedom, sustenance, paid employment, and education for their children. For the time being, however, they lived in rows of large wooden cabins divided into compartments for families. Each room contained a large fireplace, one window opening, and double-row berths against the wall for beds, benches, tables, and dippers.

Tubman spent the next two years tending to the needs of contrabands, healing wounded soldiers, and scouting the territory. She could be found at virtually any area in or around Union lines in advance of a mission, gaining as much respect for her wartime feats as she had for her Eastern Shore rescues. Union officers never failed to tip their caps when meeting her.

Shortly after the Combahee River raid, on July 18, 1863, Harriet was close enough to witness the courage of the all-black 54th Massachusetts Infantry in its fabled—and doomed—assault on Fort Wagner in Charleston Harbor. She had come to know the men of the regiment, which included Frederick Douglass's sons Lewis Henry Douglass and Charles Remond Douglass, after its arrival in Beaufort earlier in the summer. She later claimed to have served the last meal to its young white commander, Colonel Robert Gould Shaw. Tubman's description of the Battle of Fort Wagner, which resulted in 1,515 Union dead, injured, or captured, is well remembered:

And then we saw lightning, and that was the guns; and then we heard the thunder, and that was the big guns; and then we hear the rain falling, and that was drops of blood falling; and when we came to get in the crops, it was dead men that we reaped.[17]

The fighting remained intense around Charleston Harbor through September, keeping Harriet busy day and night tending to the sick and wounded. After a visit to Canada that fall to visit family, she was back in South Carolina. The commanding officer promptly ordered her to Folly Island, along the coast between Charleston and Beaufort. There, she continued her diverse duties, including intelligence gathering.

The War Winding Down

By the spring of 1864, Tubman was physically drained. She had never paid much mind to her own needs, receiving no pay and supporting herself by selling baked goods at a meager profit. On May 3, she received a letter signed by General Saxton and the surgeon in charge of the Beaufort hospital, Henry Durrant, attesting to and certifying her commitment to the sick and suffering.

The letter must have come as a great relief. Harriet was aware that black soldiers were being paid half the salary of white soldiers. Whereas white soldiers were getting $13 a month, with no clothing deductions, blacks received only $10, with $3 taken out for clothing. In protest, black soldiers refused to take any salary at all. They would help win the war and sue for full pay later. Certification and proof of service would be vital in that cause, which Tubman would join.

The black troops did not need to wait until the end of the war for fairer compensation. In June 1864, Congress finally granted equal pay to US Colored Troops and made the action retroactive. In addition, they began receiving the same rations, supplies, and medical care as white soldiers. Tubman, however, would never see any money for her service in spite of her petitions and letters written on her behalf.

86

Ever attentive to her parents' health and safety, Harriet traveled north to Auburn in the spring of 1864. Exhausted herself, she came down sick and spent months there before feeling well enough to rejoin Union forces in the Department of the South. Along the way, she was persuaded by the US Sanitary Commission—a private relief agency established to care for wounded soldiers—to report to the James River Hospitals in Virginia, where there was a pressing need for her services. It was a non-commissioned role, which may have had pay and pension repercussions she did not consider at the time, but Tubman remained there to care for sick and wounded black soldiers until July 1865.

Always more to do

By then, of course, the Confederacy had surrendered, the fighting had come to an end, and President Lincoln had been assassinated; Seward also was brutally attacked as part of the conspiracy but survived. For Harriet Tubman, this particular season of intrigue and adventure was over, though her advocacy for people mistreated or otherwise in need certainly was not.

7

Struggle to the End: "Moses" Becomes "Aunt Harriet"

"You would think that after I served the flag so faithfully, I should come to want in its folds." She looked musingly toward a nearby orchard, and she asked suddenly:
"Do you like apples?"
On being assured that I did, she said: "Did you ever plant any apple trees?"
With shame I confessed I had not.
"No," she said, "But somebody else planted them. I liked apples when I was young and I said, 'Someday I'll plant apples myself for other young folks to eat,' and I guess I did it."
—HARRIET TUBMAN, newspaper interview, 1907[1]

ORKING AT THE GOVERNMENT HOSPITAL IN VIRginia during the months immediately following the war, Harriet remained alarmed by the conditions for black soldiers. Their mortality rate was more than twice that of white soldiers in such facilities. So incensed was she by the abuses that she took up the issue with a recuperating William Seward during a visit to Washington, DC, in the summer of 1865. Seward put her in touch with the US Surgeon General, Dr. Joseph K. Barnes, who promised her the position of "Matron at the colored hospital" in Fort Monroe and the support she would need to improve conditions. But the position and the support never materialized. Tubman, clearly frustrated, dictated a strong letter that appeared in a New York publication called *The Independent*:

> *Neither the sick nor well have enough to eat; brave men die with tears in their eyes, crying for something to eat. We found great fault with the rebels for their treatment of our prisoners, but it is worse among our friends by whose aide we have fought to put down this rebellion. We could not expect much from our enemies, but from our friends we looked for justice.*[2]

Leaving Fort Monroe Hospital to return to Washington, Tubman was employed for about a month by the National Colored Home for Destitute Women and Children to "rid the asylum of the filth," as one reformer put it.[3] But conditions there remained less than sanitary, and many children died. It became clear to Harriet that the rescue of her people would take new and different forms after the war. Witnessing the conditions that took the lives of wounded black veterans, of poor and widowed black mothers, and of orphaned black children made her calling clear—the practical human needs of Reconstruction: aiding the general welfare of a people finding their place in an evolving society.

Service and Struggle

The period following the Civil War found Harriet pulled between the plight of former slaves in and around Washington, the well-being of her parents and other family members, and her own needs. In terms of her personal circumstances, the mortgage on her Auburn home needed to be paid, and the fight for her federal pension for service as a nurse, spy, and soldier had just begun. Soon came a grim lesson in the limitations of her status as a government employee and a black woman in America.

In October 1865, Harriet was heading home to be with her parents in upstate New York. As a federal employee, she was entitled to ride the train on a half-fare ticket. The conductor, however, took exception and ordered her to the smoking car. "Come, hustle out of here! We don't carry niggers for half-fare,"[4] he snarled. Tubman refused, explaining that she worked for the government and, like a soldier, could sit wherever she chose. The conductor grabbed her abruptly but, to his amazement, was unable to budge the tiny woman. With Harriet clinging stubbornly to her seat, the conductor and two passengers finally pried open her fingers, yanked her to her feet, and threw her into the smoking car. In the melee, she broke her arm and possibly some ribs. No bystanders came to her assistance as she writhed in pain all the way to New York. She would later sue the railroad company, but the case fizzled out when a witness failed to appear in court.[5]

This incident—one of many recounted in Sarah Bradford's *Scenes in the Life of Harriet Tubman* (1869), the closest thing the illiterate Tubman had to an autobiography—epitomizes the problems Harriet faced in the last fifty years of her life. Her personal strength and conviction had allowed her to take on any challenge and confront any obstacle or opponent, successfully or not. Until this point, she had lived four lives: as an enslaved African; as a one-woman rescue unit, secretly shuttling between slavery and freedom; as a spy/warrior; and, finally, as a divinely inspired caregiver and black woman seeking her full rights and status as an American. All four lives had thrust her into the contradictions of American society. And what was the reward for her selflessness, courage, and service to others?

As it was for the heroes of mythology, Tubman's reward was even more service, to be performed in the face of physical hardship, personal setback, poverty, and various forms of exploitation.

"Aunt Harriet," as she came to be called later in life, was praised by many who remembered or heard about her daring rescue missions, perpetuating her personal myth. Yet Harriet was very much a flesh-and-blood person. Like so many other female former slaves, she grew old as an illiterate, working-poor, resourceful black woman struggling to survive. The stories about her provided a measure of pride and, when they could, a little money. But they hardly provided everything she needed.

As a person who spent the first phase of her life in slavery, and the next phase risking her life to subvert and destroy it, Harriet knew the responsibilities of freedom better than any white American of her era could. She knew how to fight for what belonged to her, and battling injustice was second nature to her, no matter the railroad. Yet many battles lay ahead. She would fight to maintain her health—epitomized by brain surgery in the 1890s in which she bit on a bullet instead of taking anesthesia. She would fight for her Union pension. She would fight to maintain and expand her family. She would fight to provide food and shelter for members of her community. And she would fight to secure the right of women to vote. The costs of freedom were her oldest friends and deepest scars, and she would continue to fulfill her duties to herself and those around her to her dying breath.

The last fifty years of Harriet's life were built around four major endeavors: to protect her parents and to build and maintain a family life; to fight for her Civil War pension; to work on her biography project with Sarah H. Bradford; and to establish a home for her family and later, elderly blacks. Creating and maintaining a community both around her and for her was the fourth role and final mission in her life. Her humanitarian work and fight for justice continued throughout. She knew no other way.

Family and Marriage

Harriet settled in Auburn, where her parents and other relatives needed support. The two brothers who had been looking after them moved their families to St. Catharines. Among the others still living in the house on South Street were sister-in-law Catherine Stewart and her two children. Harriet, still suffering from her assault on the train, took charge of household affairs and found ways to support the family even though she was essentially penniless.

Harriet had fought her entire life for the safety and security of her parents, siblings, nieces, and nephews, sheltering them as best she could. Nothing would change that now. To help make ends meet, she took in boarders. She grew and sold vegetables from her garden, raised hogs in the backyard. Friends and admirers donated food and lent money when she needed it. Still, freed slaves and others passing through town who needed something to eat and a place to stay always found an open door at her house.

Harriet Tubman-Davis, her adopted daughter Gertie Davis, and Harriet's husband, Nelson Davis

Sometime in late 1867, Harriet learned that her husband, John Tubman, had been killed in an argument with a white man back in Dorchester County, Maryland, and that the murderer was acquitted by an all-white jury. Despite her estrangement from John so many years before, Harriet was both saddened and outraged by the news.

A much happier change came the following year, when she met a former slave and Civil War veteran named Nelson Davis. A boarder in her house on South Street, Davis took up work as a bricklayer in Auburn. The two fell quietly in love and married the following March at Central Presbyterian Church in town.

Nelson was twenty-two years younger than Harriet but not always in good health. They set up a brickmaking business behind the house, where Davis worked a makeshift kiln and farmed the property. He was also an active board member of the new St. Mark's AME Zion Church, founded in 1870. Harriet helped in the brickyard and garden, and hired herself out as a domestic. In 1874, the couple adopted a baby girl named Gertie; Harriet finally had a family of her own. Her marriage to Nelson lasted nearly twenty years, until his death in 1888. They battled his tuberculosis and other ailments for years.

In the meantime, Harriet's efforts to protect her parents finally came to an end as well. Her father, Ben Ross, died in 1871. Her mother Rit passed in 1879. He had likely lived into his eighties; she was in her nineties.

Pension Battle and Gold Scam

Tubman fought more than three times as long as the Civil War had lasted to get her pension for service during that conflict. The protracted struggle began in 1865, when she asked Secretary Seward for his assistance in applying for back pay. Her unofficial roles made it difficult to document her service, and the delay in equal pay for black soldiers added to the confusion.

Harriet applied for compensation again when she returned to

Auburn, only to be told that her application lacked the necessary documentation. In the years that followed, she gathered the required papers and got friends to petition the government and write letters to newspapers on her behalf. One of her admirers, New York Congressman Clinton MacDougall, introduced a bill in 1874 to get the government to act, but that effort failed as well. In 1887, Harriet petitioned Congress herself to release the file showing her back-pay application. Still nothing. Finally in 1890, after Davis's death, her application for a veteran's widow's pension was accepted. She began receiving $8 a month.

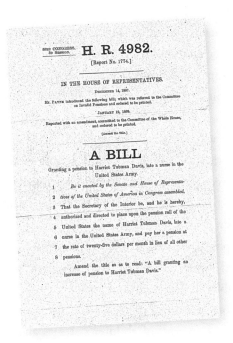

It wasn't until 1899 that Tubman would begin to receive the pension she should have been rewarded years before. No mention of retroactive pay in the bill.

Hard-working, generous, and always looking for ways to make money, Tubman and her family became easy prey for con men. In 1873, she and her brother John were approached by two men who offered them a trunk full of Confederate gold—which they claimed they found buried—said to be worth $5,000, in exchange for $2,000 in greenbacks (paper currency issued by the Treasury during the Civil War). Believing the story, Harriet borrowed $2,000 and showed in the woods to make the exchange. She ended up beaten, bound, and gagged, with no money and just a trunk full of rocks. The two men were never found.

First Biographies and Pioneering For Feminism

The support of friends and admirers for Tubman's well-being included a biography project undertaken by a well-intentioned children's writer named Sarah Hopkins Bradford. Her father, an attorney and former politician from upstate New York, had been a friend of William Seward; her brother was one of the founding pastors of Central Presbyterian Church, where Harriet was married. Bradford's motives were pure: she hoped the book would bring in a little money for Tubman and some of the recognition she deserved. All proceeds went directly to Harriet—Bradford took no royalties—and friends paid for the printing and advertising.

The biography was based heavily on interviews with Harriet herself and included stories and letters from Seward, Frederick Douglass, and other notable abolitionists and members of the Underground Railroad. Bradford attempted to be factual, telling only the stories she could verify, but as a writer of children's stories and sentimental fiction, she was largely unequipped to recount Harriet's life and exploits as they deserved to be. Much of the book is drawn from Harriet's own narration, with dialogue in slave vernacular. And while Bradford did get many of the facts right, there were also notable errors. (For example, Bradford mistakenly identifies Dr. Anthony C. Thompson as the man who owned Harriet's family.)

LETTER FROM FREDERICK DOUGLASS

The following letter, from the most prominent African American of the 19th century, accompanied the Preface to *Scenes in the Life of Harriet Tubman*. Today such a testimonial might be called a "promotional blurb" for the book.

ROCHESTER, August 29, 1868

DEAR HARRIET:

I am glad to know that the story of your eventful life has been written by a kind lady, and that the same is soon to be published. You ask for what you do not need to when you call upon me for a word of commendation. I need such words from you far more than you can need them from me, especially where your superior labors and devotion to the cause of the lately enslaved of our land are known as I know them. The difference between us is very marked. Most that I have done and suffered in the service of our cause has been in public, and I have received much encouragement at every step of the way. You [,] on the other hand [,] have labored in a private way. I have wrought in the day—you in the night. I have had the applause of the crowd and the satisfaction that comes of being approved by the multitude, while the most that you have done has been witnessed by a few trembling, scarred, and foot-sore bondsmen and women, whom you have led out of the house of bondage, and whose heartfelt "God bless you" has been your only reward. The midnight sky and the silent stars have been the witnesses of your devotion to freedom and of your heroism. Excepting John Brown—of sacred memory— I know of no one who has willingly encountered more perils and hardships to serve our enslaved people as you have . . . .[6]

The slim, 132-page biography, *Scenes in the Life of Harriet Tubman*, was published in 1869 and earned about $1,200 in proceeds. Harriet used the money to help pay off her mounting debts, including mortgage and tax payments to Seward for the Auburn house.

Scenes remains controversial, if not criticized, among Tubman scholars today for its inaccuracies and sometimes fanciful details. Nevertheless, because it was based so heavily on Tubman's own accounts, it provides the starting point for any narrative of her life. Aside from financial relief, it brought her a new level of appreciation and respect from the American public.

A revised edition of the work, under the title *Harriet, The Moses of Her People*, was issued in 1886. By this time, the promise of Reconstruction for blacks in America had been dashed and the unified nation was about to legalize Jim Crow segregation. Accordingly, the new edition of Tubman's biography was less confrontational and contained even more of her slave dialect. Omitted from it was Bradford's own essay from *Scenes*, titled "Essay on Woman-Whipping," in which she had denounced Southern women and their devotion to slavery. ("[T]he Southern mistress," she had written, "was a domestic devil with horns and claws; selfish, insolent, accustomed to be waited on for everything").[7] Omitted for the same reason was a woodcut image of Harriet as a Union soldier carrying a gun.

Given her passion for equality and injustice, it seems inevitable that Tubman would become involved in the women's suffrage movement in her later years. The women's rights movement had been established before the Civil War, but many of its strongest advocates gave first priority to the fight against slavery and had strong ties with abolitionist groups. Susan B. Anthony and others were active on the Underground Railroad, harboring fugitive slaves in their homes. After the war, the women's rights movement mobilized with the formation of major political organizations devoted to the fight for suffrage.

Tubman was never a leader of the movement, but she was an active and outspoken supporter. She attended suffragist meetings from the 1860s to the early 1900s, and went on speaking tours to recount her own experiences and advocate for equality. She said she was a member of Anthony's group, the National Women's Suffragist Association, which took a stand against the Fifteenth Amendment—

Tubman at 90 years old wearing the shawl that Queen Victoria gave to her.

guaranteeing male citizens the right to vote regardless of "race, color, or previous conditions of servitude"—because it excluded women.

The struggle for equal rights for women was particularly hard in the case of Tubman and other black suffragists because white Southern women were increasingly taking the "state's rights" line of post-Reconstruction Jim Crow racism. As Southern white women tried to push black women out of the movement, black women activists responded by forming their own national organization, the National Association of Colored Women. Harriet, introduced as "Mother Tubman," was the keynote speaker at the group's first meeting in July 1896. Mother Tubman was the oldest woman in that meeting. She had the opportunity to hold in her arms the youngest one in the meeting—the baby of Ida B. Wells-Barnett, journalist and anti-lynching activist.

Homes

With all her selfless devotion to social and humanitarian causes—and in part because of it—Harriet struggled for decades to maintain the house in Auburn. Sheltering and feeding her family members, former slaves, and others in need posed a constant challenge. She bartered with local market owners, took donations and loans from friends, and pleaded for reprieve on her loans. Proceeds from the backyard garden, brickmaking business, and sale of *Scenes in the Life* helped her to make ends meet and finally pay off the mortgage.

Then, in February 1880, the house on South Street burned to the ground. Everyone survived, but Harriet lost many priceless letters and other documents. With bricks they made themselves and more help from the community, Harriet and Nelson rebuilt the house. They continued to battle illness, however, and their financial situation remained difficult.

Harriet and Nelson's rebuilt home

None of these challenges quelled Tubman's long-held dream to create a home for the black elderly and disabled. For years, she used her house as a refuge while soliciting support in speeches and direct appeals to potential donors. A 25-acre property next to her house on

South Street was put up for auction in 1896, and Harriet won with a bid of $1,450. Asked how she was going to pay for the property, Harriet allegedly said, "I'm going home to tell the Lord Jesus all about it."[8]

Her brother William Henry Stewart loaned money for the down payment, and a local bank granted a mortgage of $1,000. The venture was incorporated as the Harriet Tubman Home, Inc., and its namesake continued to solicit support and to house those in need while construction proceeded. Mounting debt and tax obligations finally led the AME Zion Church to take over the property—a welcome development for all—and the dream was finally realized with the opening of the Harriet Tubman Home for Aged and Infirmed Negroes in 1908.

Death and Burial

Still plagued by headaches and seizures—and undergoing brain surgery for them in the late 1890s—Harriet became increasingly frail. The most active and nimble of persons in her younger years, she adjusted to life in a wheelchair beginning in about 1910. As her grandniece, Alice Brickler, reported years later to biographer Earl Conrad, Tubman was undiminished in spirit. During one childhood visit, Brickler wrote, her aunt playfully slid off her wheelchair and followed her into the garden like a snake.

> So smoothly did it glide and with so little noise. I was frightened! Then reason conquered fear and I knew it was Aunt Harriet, flat on her stomach and with only the use of her arms and serpentine movements of her body, gliding smoothly along. Mother helped her back to her chair and they laughed. Aunt Harriet then told me that was the way she had gone by many a sentinel during the war.[9]

By 1911, Tubman was bedridden and so frail that there was no choice but to move her to the home next door. Friends and admirers once again came to her assistance, raising the funds to pay for her care.

Pneumonia finally took Harriet's life on March 10, 1913. She was days away from what was likely her 91st birthday. According to black activist Mary Talbert, among those gathered in the room at the time of her passing, Tubman quoted from the Book of John (14:3) before falling into a coma: "I go away to prepare a place for you, that where I am you also may be."

Two memorial services were held on March 13, one at the Tubman Home and one at the Thompson Memorial AME Zion Church. Both were attended by hundreds of mourners, with additional crowds gathered in between to view her body. An American flag draped her casket, with a crucifix in her hands and a silver medal she had received from Queen Victoria inside. She was buried with military honors at Fort Hill Cemetery in Auburn, next to family members.

The communities to which Harriet belonged were determined to leave public markers attesting to her remarkable life. One, thanks to Mary Talbert, was a monument at her gravesite. Another, unveiled a year after her death and later mounted on the county courthouse, was a bronze tablet inscribed with her likeness and a testimonial that reads in part:

WITH IMPLICIT TRUST IN GOD,
SHE BRAVED EVERY DANGER AND
OVERCAME EVERY OBSTACLE, WITHAL
SHE POSSESSED EXTRAORDINARY
FORESIGHT AND JUDGMENT SO THAT
SHE TRUTHFULLY SAID—
"ON MY UNDERGROUND RAILROAD,
I NEBBER RUN MY TRAIN OFF DE TRACK
AND I NEBBER LOS A PASSENGER."

8

Harriet and the Land of Freedom

> *"God's time is always near. He set the North Star in the heavens; He gave me the strength in my limbs; He meant I should be free."* —HARRIET TUBMAN

STUDENTS OF THE ALBANY (NY) FREE SCHOOL HAD completed a 13-day trip tracing the path of the Underground Railroad when they met with US Senator Hillary Clinton in 2002. They only had one question for her: Why was Harriet Tubman never paid her pension in full?

Senator Clinton took the question to heart and introduced a bill that secured funding to repay Harriet Tubman's Civil War pension. In October 2003, after her bill was passed, the US government sent $11,750 to the Harriet Tubman Home in Auburn, NY. The funds would be used to maintain the facility and honor Tubman's memory. Said Clinton:

I thank the Albany students who brought this matter to my attention last year and I am proud that we can now honor the memory of Harriet

Tubman by making sure that this injustice is remedied. Harriet Tubman was one of our nation's most courageous freedom fighters. It is important that we officially recognize her extraordinary service.

Harriet would have been grateful to see the home maintained and to know that all her efforts in the name of freedom—along with those of other abolitionists and everyone who participated in the Underground Railroad—were not forgotten. She would have been proud as well of the young students who stood up for fairness and raised the issue of her pension.

In her youthful dreams of freedom, as she flew over fields, towns, and mountains away from her life of bondage, Harriet conjured a gathering of ladies in white who would reach out and take her in. Much as her Ashanti ancestors might have inferred, Harriet came to expect that helping hands would be there when she reached freedom up North. In reality, when the scared teenage runaway finally landed in Philadelphia in the fall of 1849, there was no one to lend a hand. "I had crossed the line," she recounted. "I was free; but there was no one to welcome me to the land of freedom. I was a stranger in a strange land. . . ."[2]

That dream and that reality are emblematic of the African American experience. Black people—especially women—who struggle against white supremacy gain many acquaintances and admirers, but few true friends and allies. That is because, historically, it has been dangerous to be true friends and allies of any oppressed people. Tubman's colleagues on the Underground Railroad, black and white, were aberrations, heretics of their time. Not only did they believe in the humanity of all people, but they mobilized and organized to act on that belief and risked—in some cases lost—their lives in doing so.

The line between slavery and freedom, thought and action, has existed throughout time. Again and again in the course of world history, challengers have emerged to find and cross that barrier, then destroy it. Tubman found many who were willing to help her because she was willing to help herself—to take the first step toward the line and the next step over it. Then she spent the rest of her life helping others help themselves, inspiring ordinary individuals to help the less fortunate. By her efforts and example, she led people beyond their personal and collective boundaries.

Minty.

Moses.

General Tubman.

Aunt Harriet.

So many lives—too many in which to find just one lesson. In order to properly assess and appreciate Harriet Tubman in the 21st century, there are at least four things we should know.

I. Harriet was not a superhero, or an American folklore figure like Paul Bunyan or John Henry. She was a real human being. She was a poor, illiterate black woman who struggled to maintain her family and community of friends and allies. She accomplished more than most people because she was more courageous than most people. Her courage inspired others to rise to the challenges of the time. Her profound faith allowed her to transform herself into a person who could accomplish, by any practical standard, miracles.

Tubman's story, in the end, is not just the story of the power of the American spirit; it is not just another uplifting narrative of an individual overcoming adversity. Hers is a story of how real transformations of society come from a fundamentally unselfish place—one that balances great pain, great hope, and great perseverance. And one without earthly reward.

Stripped of childish sentiment, Harriet's story reminds us that human beings are much more powerful than they often choose to be. That reminder is important because working for freedom in a society that actively—sometimes violently—restricts it for some citizens can still carry grave consequences, no matter where or when the freedom-seeker takes up the cause. Harriet Tubman belongs in the pantheon of the world's human rights champions whose example, we can only hope, will continue to inspire others in the 21st century.

2. Since the time of slavery, black women have been—and remain—the glue that holds black American society together. In a nation that enslaved, lynched, and disenfranchised black men, black women had to step up for the race to survive. Harriet Tubman not only stepped up, but she stepped forward—past most of the people of her time, black or white, male or female. She advanced the cause of abolition as a leader of the Underground Railroad, a supporter of John Brown's raid on Harpers Ferry, and an active contributor to the Union military campaign.

The advantage of black women who take leadership roles is that no one in power ever considers them a threat to the white male status quo. Nineteenth-century black women like Harriet Tubman, Sojourner Truth, and Jarena Lee, the first authorized female preacher in the AME Church, spoke out boldly at a time when women were discouraged, even prohibited, from speaking in public at all. If she were alive today, Tubman would be pleased but not surprised to learn that Black Lives Matter—the loose confederation of black activists who campaign against violence and social injustice toward the African American community—was started by a small group of black women. Tubman is a North Star in her own right, as black women today continue to invoke her name when discussing the leadership example of women activists of the past.

3. Mainstream America accepts black heroes only if they are perceived as nonviolent. Harriet Tubman carried a pistol as she made her trips back and forth between "Egypt" and the "Promised Land"; no doubt she had a rifle on raids and scouting missions during the Civil War. Yet we have no record of her using a weapon and no evidence of her ever killing or harming a white person. And so Harriet is perceived as a "safe" figure in black history, with a safe story. Would she be the celebrated figure that she is—memorialized on the $20 bill—if she had actually participated in John Brown's raid or if she had killed white slave owners the way Nat Turner, another devout Christian who led a slave insurrection, did?[3]

> "The story is as old as time, but it is contemporary. These revolutionaries left us with a blueprint to move forward and to find our own acts of activism" and "to find that healing mechanism."
> —ANTHONY HEMINGWAY,
> executive producer, *Underground*
> (WGN cable network drama about the Underground Railroad)

4. Being "Harriet Tubman" was a conscious choice she made. She could have remained in Pennsylvania after gaining her freedom and never left. She could have devoted her life to obtaining an education, building a quiet life for herself, and enjoying her freedom. Or she could have gotten her family out of the South and then stopped. Instead, Harriett made a conscious choice—again and again—to risk her life in the effort to rescue people from bondage. She actively decided to provide a home for her family and members of her community. And she was determined to create a refuge for the aged and infirmed. She was one person who made a difference because she was more concerned with others than she was with herself—because she made that choice and sacrificed for it throughout her life, both before and after slavery, far more than she might have.

The lives of Harriet Tubman are just beginning to get the attention they deserve. Her reputation continues to grow, as she gains recognition as one of the most inspiring and impactful social-change agents the United States has produced. Others say, more succinctly, that with the help of God, an enslaved African woman who was denied her basic humanity by a racist society, decided to re-create herself.

Reborn as a Spirit Guide of black and female independence, she left enduring examples of courage, service, the true responsibilities of American citizenship, and, ultimately, humanity itself. Those examples have taken her far beyond the line that separates obscurity and eternity.

And she is still leading only the bravest to freedom.

Acknowledgments

Though this is not a religious book, my inspiration and research were driven by Harriet Tubman's own spiritual wisdom and faith. Her intuitiveness, inner strength, and dedication to freedom clearly derived from her belief in a higher power, and I take this moment to honor that same force. I believe God is the reason all the pieces came together in this project.

Foremost among those pieces—and objects of my gratitude—is my friend, the journalist and historian Dr. Todd Steven Burroughs, who offered everything from his expertise to his connection with the publisher. Our long discussions about the real Harriet Tubman and her impact on society and culture were invaluable. This book would not be the same without him.

I am profoundly grateful as well to the groundbreaking historian and Tubman biographer Dr. Kate Larson, to whom I first reached out with a question about details of the enslaved people that Tubman freed. Kate ended up reading and correcting the full manuscript, and I cannot thank her enough.

To Jeff Hacker, Merrilee Warholak, and Dawn Reshen-Doty of For Beginners, thank you for taking a chance on this Newark, NJ, schoolteacher who was intent on not letting you down.

Illustrator Lynsey Hutchinson took on the challenge of creating the images for this book, and she did so with absolute passion from the start. There were times, especially as we approached the final deadline, that I pushed the limits, but she handled every request and suggestion with true grace and professionalism. My gratitude as well to Susan

Ades Stone for her insightful and context-setting foreword.

Closer to home, I extend special thanks to my cousin, the one and only, playwright-actor Karen Jones-Meadows, whose one-woman theatrical production, *Harriet's Return*, first put Harriet Tubman in our family consciousness and DNA. Karen also lent me the Earl Conrad biography (*General Harriet Tubman*) she used in her own research. Maybe by the time this book is published, she will have Conrad back.

And finally, thanks again to Mom and Dad, for making sure I was able to sign my name on my first library card. Without that card, I could not have checked out my first book on Harriet Tubman and so many others.

Notes

Chapter 1

[1] Lapham, Stephen H., and Hanes, Peter, "Harriet Tubman: Emancipate Yourself!" *Social Studies and the Young Learner* 25 no. 4 (May–June 2013). National Council for the Social Studies.

[2] Telford, Emma P. *Harriet: The Modern Moses of Heroism and Vision*, as quoted in Larson, Kate Clifford, *Bound for the Promised Land: Harriet Tubman, Portrait of an American Hero*. New York: Ballantine, 2003, p. 21.

Chapter 2

[1] Bradford, Sarah H. *Scenes in the Life of Harriet Tubman*. Auburn, NY: W.J. Moses, 1869, p. 14 (http://docsouth.unc.edu/neh/bradford/bradford.html).

[2] Ibid., p. 15.

[3] Ibid., p. 15.

[4] Ibid., p. 20.

Chapter 3

[1] Foner, Eric. *Gateway to Freedom: The Hidden Story of the Underground Railroad*. New York: W.W. Norton, 2015, p. 16.

[2] Hodges, Graham Russell. *David Ruggles: A Radical Black Abolitionist and the Underground Railroad in New York City*. Chapel Hill: University of North Carolina Press, 2010.

[3] Douglass, Frederick. *Life and Times of Frederick Douglass*. Hartford,

CT: Park Publishing, 1881, p. 271 (http://docsouth.unc.edu/neh/douglasslife/douglass.html).

[4] Still, William. *The Underground Railroad: Authentic Narratives and First-Hand Accounts.* Mineola, NY: Dover, 2007. Original edition published in Philadelphia by Porter and Coates, 1872.

[5] Ibid.

[6] Ibid.

[7] Bradford, Sarah H. *Harriet, The Moses of Her People.* New York: George R. Lockwood & Son, 1886, p. 60 (http://docsouth.unc.edu/neh/harriet/harriet.html).

[8] Bradford, *Scenes in the Life of Harriet Tubman*, p. 33–34.

[9] Ibid., p. 62.

[10] Widely quoted, from a suffrage convention in New York, 1896.

Chapter 4

[1] Brown, William Wells. *The Rising Son.* Boston: A.G. Brown, 1873, p. 538 (archive.org/details/risingsonorantec00brow).

[2] Still, William. *The Underground Railroad.* Philadelphia, 1886, p. 297.

[3] Ibid.

[4] www.harriet-tubman.org/letter-by-thomas-garrett.

[5] Humez, Jean M. *Harriet Tubman: The Life and the Life Stories.* Madison: University of Wisconsin Press, 2003.

[6] The Old Testament story of Ham, one of the three sons of Noah (with Shem and Japheth) has been used at times to justify white supremacy. In the Book of Genesis (9:20–27), Noah puts a curse on Ham's descendants, starting with Canaan, because he saw his drunken father naked. The supposedly black-skinned Canaanites, according to the story, were cursed to become servants to Shem's descendants. For centuries, white Christian denominations in Europe and later North America used this story to explain the origin of

black-skinned people and their God-ordained servitude.

[7] Chapter 6, verse 5 of the New Testament's Book of Ephesians contains a favorite quote of slavemasters, which drilled into the minds of their human chattel: "Slaves, obey your earthly masters with respect and fear, and with sincerity of heart, just as you would obey Christ."

[8] Still, William. *The Underground Railroad*. www.gutenberg.org/files/15263/15263-h/15263-h.htm#bhross. The Rosses were exposed to a variety of Christian denominations. The Pattisons, Thompsons, and Brodesses had belonged to the Episcopal Church before becoming Methodist. The Rosses may have been Catholic before becoming Methodist and appear to have been influenced by the Baptist Church as well.

[9] Larson, p. 43.

[10] Humez, p. 234, quoting Thomas Garrett, 1868.

[11] Bradford, *Scenes in the Life of Harriet Tubman*, p. 79.

[12] Ibid., p. 20.

[13] The Robert Moss Blog. Mossdreams.blogspot.com (http://mossdreams.blogspot.com/2011/09/harriet-tubman-and-leopard-dreaming.html).

[14] Bradford, *Scenes in the Life of Harriet Tubman*, p. 80.

[15] Bradford, *Harriet, The Moses of Her People*, p. 92–93.

Chapter 5

[1] Letter to John Holmes, April 22, 1820 (www.loc.gov/exhibits/jefferson/159.html).

[2] Quoted in Goodrich, Thomas. *War to the Knife: Bleeding Kansas, 1854–1861*. Lincoln: University of Nebraska Press, 2004, p. 8.

[3] First quoted in Richard Josiah Hinton. *John Brown and His Men; With Some Account of the Roads They Traveled to Reach Harper's Ferry*. New York: Funk & Wagnalls, 1894, p. 135.

[4] Larson, p. 157–158.

[5] Horwitz, Tony. *Midnight Rising: John Brown and the Raid That Sparked the Civil War.* New York: Henry Holt, 2004, p. 42.

[6] Conrad, Earl. *General Harriet Tubman.* Originally printed in 1943. Washington, DC: The Associated Publishers, p. 124.

[7] Quoted in Larson, p. 177.

Chapter 6

[1] From an address in Rochester, New York, April 28, 1861, as quoted in Louis P. Masur, ed., *The Real War Will Never Get in the Books: Selections from Writers During the Civil War.* New York: Oxford University Press, 1993, pg. 101.

[2] Quoted in Conrad, p. 136.

[3] *The New York Times*, May 1, 1860.

[4] Larson, p. 184.

[5] http://www.nytimes.com/learning/general/onthisday/harp/1224.html

[6] *The Liberator*, February 21, 1861, as cited in Larson, p. 361.

[7] Freed Men & Southern Society Project. http://www.freedmen.umd.edu/hunter.htm#HUNTER

[8] Ibid.

[9] Quoted in Conrad, p. 157

[10] Bradford. *Harriet, The Moses of Her People*, p. 141

[11] Humez, p. 302

[12] Letter on March 21, 1868, as quoted in Bradford, *Harriet, The Moses of Her People*, p. 142.

[13] Catherine Clinton. *Harriet Tubman: The Road to Freedom.* Boston: Little Brown, 2004, p. 166.

[14] Larson, p. 216.

[15] *Wisconsin State Journal*, June 6, 1863, as quoted in Clinton, p. 215.

¹⁶ Ibid, p. 216.

¹⁷ Humez, p. 135.

Chapter 7

¹ *The New York Herald*, September 22, 1907. Interview with Frank C. Drake.

² Harriet Tubman, "Soldiers Dying from Hunger and Neglect: A Woman's Appeal," *The Independent . . . Devoted to the Consideration of Politics, Social and Economic Tendencies, History, Literature and the Arts* (New York), July 27, 1863, reproduced in Oertel, Kristen T. *Harriet Tubman: Slavery, the Civil War, and Civil Rights in the 19th Century.* New York: Routledge, 2016, p. 74.

³ Colman, Lucy N. *Reminiscences.* Buffalo, NY: H.L. Green, 1891, p. 63. (https://archive.org/stream/reminiscencescolm#page/n7/mode/2up)

⁴ Bradford, *Scenes in the Life of Harriet Tubman*, p. 46. The following year, African American suffragist Francis Ellen Wilkins Harper would tell the National Women's Rights Convention in New York City that she had suffered similar abuse on a Washington–Baltimore train for refusing to sit in the smoking car. Ida B. Wells, a Memphis schoolteacher who would become one of black America's most famous 19th-century journalists, would famously suffer similar mistreatment in 1884.

⁵ Larson, 232–233.

⁶ Bradford, *Scenes in the Life of Harriet Tubman*, p.6–7

⁷ Ibid, p. 122–123.

⁸ Larson, 280

⁹ Alice Lucas Brickler to Earl Conrad, July 28, 1939. Earl Conrad/Harriet Tubman Collection, New York Public Library, Schomburg Center for Research in Black Culture. As quoted in Larson, p. 288.

Chapter 8

[1] http://www.harriettubman.com/senclintion.html.

[2] Bradford, 20.

[3] Milton C. Sernett points out how Tubman's public image was largely determined by white abolitionists: "Tubman's story transcends the limitation of the biblical parallel of Moses. Her military service during the Civil War resonates more with the figure of Joshua than Moses. When piloting scared fugitives out of slavery's prison, Tubman is said to have carried a gun. Most white abolitionists drank deeply from the well of nonviolence; this was especially true of the Garrisonians [followers of William Lloyd Garrison] in the Boston clique of abolitionists. Had Tubman's reputation as a liberator been forged, as was Nat Turner's, in the school of blood and violence, she might not have been embraced as the Moses of the Underground Railroad. In the wake of John Brown's attack on Harpers Ferry, some abolitionists, including Franklin B. Sanborn, architect of that early Tubman iconic representation [as Moses], jettisoned older notions of nonresistance to evil and took up a philosophy of righteous violence. In their minds, the Civil War was a cleansing fire, purging out the dross of slavery. Their 'Black Moses' must also be a warrior." (*Harriet Tubman: Myth, Memory, and History*. Durham, NC: Duke University Press, 2007, p. 72)

About the Author

ANNETTE ALSTON is a longtime educator in the Newark (NJ) public school system and has served as president of the Newark Teachers' Association. Her writings have appeared in the *New York Amsterdam News*, *NJEA Review*, and *NJEA Reporter*; her series on the 25th anniversary of the 1967 Newark rebellion won a National Newspaper Publishers Association (NNPA) Merit Award. Annette has a B.A. in journalism from Rutgers University–New Brunswick and an M.A. in Social Studies from Concordia University.

About the Illustrator

LYNSEY HUTCHINSON is a freelance illustrator and musician from Edinburgh, Scotland. Her work was first published in the award-winning graphic novel *Burke & Hare* (Insomnia 2009) alongside such celebrated artists as Frank Quitely and Rian Hughes. She is one of the creators behind the Southern Gothic anthology *Bayou Arcana: Songs of Loss and Redemption* (Markosia 2012) contributing the strip 'Grinder Blues.' Both Lynsey and her artwork appeared in the BAFTA-nominated 2011 independent Scottish film *Electric Man*. You can check out her illustrations and music at www.thehoudinibox.com

THE FOR BEGINNERS® SERIES

www.forbeginnersbooks.com

THE FOR BEGINNERS® SERIES

THE HISTORY OF OPERA FOR BEGINNERS	ISBN 978-1-934389-79-9
ISLAM FOR BEGINNERS	ISBN 978-1-934389-01-0
JANE AUSTEN FOR BEGINNERS	ISBN 978-1-934389-61-4
JUNG FOR BEGINNERS	ISBN 978-1-934389-76-8
KIERKEGAARD FOR BEGINNERS	ISBN 978-1-934389-14-0
LACAN FOR BEGINNERS	ISBN 978-1-934389-39-3
LIBERTARIANISM FOR BEGINNERS	ISBN 978-1-939994-66-0
LINCOLN FOR BEGINNERS	ISBN 978-1-934389-85-0
LINGUISTICS FOR BEGINNERS	ISBN 978-1-934389-28-7
LITERARY THEORY FOR BEGINNERS	ISBN 978-1-939994-60-8
MALCOLM X FOR BEGINNERS	ISBN 978-1-934389-04-1
MARX'S DAS KAPITAL FOR BEGINNERS	ISBN 978-1-934389-59-1
MCLUHAN FOR BEGINNERS	ISBN 978-1-934389-75-1
MORMONISM FOR BEGINNERS	ISBN 978-1-939994-52-3
MUSIC THEORY FOR BEGINNERS	ISBN 978-1-939994-46-2
NIETZSCHE FOR BEGINNERS	ISBN 978-1-934389-05-8
PAUL ROBESON FOR BEGINNERS	ISBN 978-1-934389-81-2
PHILOSOPHY FOR BEGINNERS	ISBN 978-1-934389-02-7
PLATO FOR BEGINNERS	ISBN 978-1-934389-08-9
POETRY FOR BEGINNERS	ISBN 978-1-934389-46-1
POSTMODERNISM FOR BEGINNERS	ISBN 978-1-934389-09-6
PRISON INDUSTRIAL COMPLEX FOR BEGINNERS	ISBN 978-1-939994-31-8
PROUST FOR BEGINNERS	ISBN 978-1-939994-44-8
RELATIVITY & QUANTUM PHYSICS FOR BEGINNERS	ISBN 978-1-934389-42-3
SARTRE FOR BEGINNERS	ISBN 978-1-934389-15-7
SAUSSURE FOR BEGINNERS	ISBN 978-1-939994-41-7
SHAKESPEARE FOR BEGINNERS	ISBN 978-1-934389-29-4
STANISLAVSKI FOR BEGINNERS	ISBN 978-1-939994-35-6
STRUCTURALISM & POSTSTRUCTURALISM FOR BEGINNERS	ISBN 978-1-934389-10-2
TESLA FOR BEGINNERS	ISBN 978-1-939994-48-6
TONI MORRISON FOR BEGINNERS	ISBN 978-1-939994-54-7
WOMEN'S HISTORY FOR BEGINNERS	ISBN 978-1-934389-60-7
UNIONS FOR BEGINNERS	ISBN 978-1-934389-77-5
U.S. CONSTITUTION FOR BEGINNERS	ISBN 978-1-934389-62-1
ZEN FOR BEGINNERS	ISBN 978-1-934389-06-5
ZINN FOR BEGINNERS	ISBN 978-1-934389-40-9

www.forbeginnersbooks.com